BE MONEY SMART

BE MONEY SMART

*A Practical Guide for Starting Out,
Starting Over, and Staying on Track*

FARNOOSH TORABI

Vice President, Publisher: Tim Moore
Associate Publisher and Director of Marketing: Amy Neidlinger
Executive Editor: Jeanne Glasser
Editorial Assistant: Pamela Boland
Development Editor: Russ Hall
Senior Marketing Manager: Julie Phifer
Assistant Marketing Manager: Megan Graue
Cover Designer: Alan Clements
Managing Editor: Kristy Hart
Project Editor: Betsy Harris
Copy Editor: Keith Cline
Proofreader: Water Crest Publishing
Indexer: Lisa Stumpf
Interior Designer: Gloria Schurick
Senior Compositor: Gloria Schurick
Manufacturing Buyer: Dan Uhrig

© 2012 by Farnoosh Torabi
Published by Pearson Education, Inc.
Publishing as FT Press
Upper Saddle River, New Jersey 07458

FT Press offers excellent discounts on this book when ordered in quantity for bulk purchases or special sales. For more information, please contact U.S. Corporate and Government Sales, 1-800-382-3419, corpsales@pearsontechgroup.com. For sales outside the U.S., please contact International Sales at international@pearson.com.

Printed in the United States of America

First Printing October 2011

ISBN-10: 0-13-288806-8
ISBN-13: 978-0-13-288806-6

Pearson Education LTD.
Pearson Education Australia PTY, Limited.
Pearson Education Singapore, Pte. Ltd.
Pearson Education North Asia, Ltd.
Pearson Education Canada, Ltd.
Pearson Educación de Mexico, S.A. de C.V.
Pearson Education—Japan
Pearson Education Malaysia, Pte. Ltd.

Library of Congress Cataloging-in-Publication Data

Torabi, Farnoosh.

Be money smart : a practical guide for starting out, starting over, and staying on track / Farnoosh Torabi.

p. cm.

Includes index.

ISBN-13: 978-0-13-288806-6 (pbk. : alk. paper)

ISBN-10: 0-13-288806-8 (pbk. : alk. paper)

1. Finance, Personal—Psychological aspects. 2. Money—Psychological aspects. 3. Financial security. I. Title.

HG179.T5925 2011

332.024—dc23

2011037077

2 V036 11

For my family

Contents

PART II   Psych It Up

PART III   Raise the Bar

Acknowledgments

I have the great fortune of knowing encouraging and inspiring individuals who've made my career and life an absolute joy, in addition to having helped spring my ideas and this book to life.

Thank you to my superb agent, Adam Kirschner, who pushed for this project, just as I was about to give up hope. Thank you to the very supportive and talented Pearson team: Jeanne Glasser, Tim Moore, and Julie Phifer. Thank you all for rallying behind me and reminding me to always think big. Boom!

This book could not have been possible without the generosity and brilliance of behavioral experts, teachers, and economists who shared with me their perspectives, theories, and thoughts. Thank you especially to the great Dan Ariely, Jay Ritter, Terri Ciochetti, and Joseph Brusuelas.

I am enormously grateful to the television producers who have allowed me to share my perspectives on their airwaves. First and foremost, Patricia Luchsinger, a magnificent producer at the NBC *Today Show*, who was the first person to take a serious chance on me and put me on live, national TV at a young age. Thanks for the big break and for inviting me back. Thank you to the excellent Katherine Billman, also from the *Today Show*. Thank you to all the brave and inspiring participants on *Bank of Mom & Dad*. And of course, monstrous thanks to my *Bank of Mom & Dad* family at ABC Daytime and BBC America who helped bring this very important program to life: Ann Miller, Lillian Lim, Marianne Fleschman, Allison Wallach, Bob Kirsh, Shirley Escott, Jerry Kolber, and Tracey Finley.

My deepest gratitude to all the individuals with whom I've had the opportunity to collaborate in the past year, who've helped me extend my reach in educating everyday people about money. I'm especially thankful for Christine Schirmer, Jen Garcia, Jen Fellner, Scott Gulbransen, Chelsea Marti, Kathryn Zambito, Courtney Leddy, Chris Lee, Kathleen McGraw, Katie Grafer, Denise Vitola, Kristen Ronan, Colleen McCarthy, and Naomi Borno.

I have wonderful friends who keep me brave: Kate Dailey, Bethany and Tim McGee, Ariel Gornizky, Kathryn Ricker, Tim Chan, Kafi Drexel, Margie Fox, Brian Maloney, David Dapko, Annika, Michael, Luke, and Blake O'Looney, Susan, Michael, Allison, and Amanda Beacham, Kathy Braddock, Kelly and Eric Tiedeken, Christine and Mike Rzasa, Tim Hedden, Kristin Bentz, Susie Banikarim, and Dan Arnall. Thanks to all of you for your unconditional friendship and support.

Thank you to Dean Jim Thomas and Joyce Matthews and the entire Smeal College of Business at Pennsylvania State University, my alma mater.

A great thank you to my Lancaster, PA family for their love and support: Eileen and Phil Jaquith; Kate Dussinger; and Doug, Jean, and Bradley Dussinger.

Speaking of family, much love and a great big thank you to Aunt Sheren, Uncle Nasser, and my AZ cousins Alex and Allen.

Thank you to Adam and Sheila Torabi, my amazing parents—to whom I owe pretty much my entire life. The greatest gift they ever gave me—besides guidance, unconditional love, and trust—was my brother Todd back in 1991. With Todd, there is inspiration and joy. And the future always seems brighter.

Finally, I am blessed for my best friend and steady Tim Dussinger. Thank you for all the all.

About the Author

Farnoosh Torabi is a personal finance expert, author, speaker, and TV personality. *The New York Times* calls her advice "perfectly practical." Her first book, *You're So Money*, was widely acclaimed for its candid, tell-all advice for young adults seeking financial independence.

Farnoosh's latest television work includes SOAPnet's *Bank of Mom & Dad*, where she coaches young women struggling with debt. She was also the resident finance expert on TLC's *REAL SIMPLE. REAL LIFE*.

You've seen Farnoosh on *Larry King Live, The View, Today, Good Morning America, The Early Show, Tyra, Fox News, MSNBC*, and *CNN*. She was formerly a Senior Financial Correspondent and host of *Wall Street Confidential* with Jim Cramer for TheStreet.com TV.

Farnoosh's work and advice have been profiled in *The New York Times, The New York Post, Real Simple, Glamour, Marie Claire, Seventeen, Cosmopolitan, Money Magazine, AOL, People*, and *Entrepreneur Magazine*.

Farnoosh attended Pennsylvania State University, graduating with honors in finance and international business. She also holds an M.S. in journalism from Columbia University.

Preface

The arrival of this book and its message, I suspect, could not have been better timed. We're more than two years into this great recession, and many of us are more confused than ever about our personal finances. With the financial and employment landscapes evolving before us, it's difficult to return to the old, prescriptive advice we've grown accustomed to. Emotionally, we've got a lot going on; we're angry, hurt, confused, and we've lost confidence. Our emotions have (and continue to) run high. By now we recognize that we need to change our ways, but not in a knee-jerk, reactionary way. After all, economic volatility is cyclical and will likely return in a new form in the near future. What's needed is advice that doesn't just stem from the rules and regulations of the banking, credit, and financial world but is rooted in our behavior and habits. We need to understand ourselves, get honest, and make money one of the most personal issues and biggest priorities of our lives. If we can get a tighter hold on our minds, our actions, and our belief systems, we can be in control of anything, most importantly our financial lives.

When I first started developing this book, I struggled to succinctly describe its idea to my colleagues, friends, and family. Not because I hadn't a clue, but because my mind was racing. Only until I was deep into my writing could I possibly narrow it down, and even then my summary ran wild. "It's about how our emotions complicate our financial lives and hinder us from making the best financial decisions…It's about the complications of money and how it's actually never about the money…*ramble ramble ramble*…It's about how we have the ability to make better financial decisions, but rarely do…It's…well, it's complicated," went my usual rant (followed by awkward silence). My sympathetic listeners often responded with generous nods and smiles. They said they couldn't wait to read it, even though they weren't quite sure what the heck I was talking about!

This book has been an incredible learning process and has been, by far, my most challenging project. It's been a couple years since I've authored a book. The first was a financial guide for young adults, and as my readers and I matured, we reached a place where we demanded a deeper understanding and explanation of money. We wanted to get a better handle on our financial commitments and our future goals. We wanted to better understand our mistakes and learn how to lay a foundation for personal wealth down the road, especially with the recent financial crisis. This book teaches us how to stop second-guessing ourselves, how to differentiate what is financially right and wrong, and how to actually make the best decisions on our own terms.

Fortunately, I've always had a deep curiosity for understanding why we do the silly things we do with money, so researching the *why* for this book was quite entertaining at times. The behavioral research was available in abundance, thanks to some economic pioneers. Without them and their brilliant minds, this book would be just 50% complete. As for me, my promise was to provide the *what now* to readers. What do we do, now that we know we have irrational tendencies when it comes to money? How do we actually begin to embrace the *M* word in a more honest, personal, and rational way?

Finding solutions to these questions has been a journey of discovery. Looking back, it was a trip I believe that was launched long before I began developing the notion behind *Be Money Smart*. It started when I began entering people's homes, watching them spend money and hearing them talk about their goals. There's nothing like the face to face. Participating in shows such as TLC's *Real Simple. Real Life* and SOAPnet's *Bank of Mom & Dad* allowed me to see and hear actual people struggling with money. Through them, I discovered how our emotions and our biases can deeply influence our financial decisions. And getting to the root of your emotions—and realizing you can control them—is the first *what now* step toward financial freedom. Along the way, I've learned and taught that financial freedom is also about respecting yourself, having a deep understanding of what you want and *don't* want in life, and of course, living within your means.

In the chapters that follow, I'll help you develop the discipline, behaviors, and habits that will lead you to make positive choices about your financial life. I'll help you dig into what's keeping you from being motivated and taking positive action, and look at the behaviors that make people "money zombies." Once those ingrained behaviors are exposed, we can explore the positive habits and the discipline necessary to build a secure financial future.

The methods in this book will enable you to pursue personal and professional goals and will result in achieving financial security, now, five years from now, and long into the future.

Your journey starts now.

Introduction

Being decisive about money can be a crapshoot. By the time you finish reading this book, you'll find out why and what you can do about it.

Ask yourself: Why is it that even the best, most coherent and logical financial advice does little to mobilize us into thinking about or taking control of our money in a meaningful way? Rarely does a lecture on retirement savings and life insurance inspire us to build a path toward improved security and financial well-being. When it comes to making decisive financial choices, there's a visible disconnect between our mind and our actions.

Between earning money and spending lies a world of uncertainty—a gray area. We lose sleep over finding the right answers to questions such as: *How do I afford my student loans? When is the right time to buy a house? Where is my money best invested? Why can't I kick the credit card habit? How do I budget for uncertain times? Why do I make impulsive purchases? What was I thinking when I bought this Vespa? And why do I feel the need to keep giving money to mooching friends? Why, when I know better?*

Do you see yourself up there in that swirl of hows, whys, and wheres?

This book is based on the principal that our financial lives—much like life in general—are powered and transformed by personal choices and behaviors, both of which are rooted in our values, perspectives, goals, and financial means. Rarely, though, do we really consider all these key variables when making a purchase, investing in stocks, building savings, or charging against a credit card. Sometimes we just look at price tags and shrug in compliance, or perhaps we're so narrow-minded about our goals we miss great financial opportunities. In other cases, we can't even get to the point of making any decisions. We feel paralyzed and stop dead in our tracks. Emotions prevent us from getting the right help. So instead, poor decisions are made, or worse, nothing at all is done.

A Behavioral Bubble

You can blame your emotions; they play an enormous role when we attempt to manage our personal finances. Many behavioral experts will go so far as to say that our emotions can potentially *destroy* the ability to make sound financial moves. Finance and economic experts, including Curtis Faith and Dan Ariely (both best-selling authors), have told me that human behavior played a great role in, for example, the Great Recession. Many were caught in a "behavioral bubble"— thinking and acting irrationally, expecting that home prices would rise generously year after year.

We're only human, right? Jay Ritter, the Cordell Professor of Finance at the University of Florida and an expert on behavioral finance, told me that he believes we are all afflicted by "cognitive biases." Translation: mental barriers. We lean toward following easy, but not always helpful, rules of thumb. Some individuals are overconfident about their decision-making abilities, which can manifest in investing excessively and not asking for help when it's really needed.

According to Ritter, we tend to rely more on short-term rather than long-term patterns, which can prove detrimental when making decisions that concern certain financial moves like investing in the stock market or buying real estate. "People tend to put too much weight on recent experiences," says Ritter. In addition to recency bias, another behavioral tendency that plagues us is "group think." Humans are prone to trusting conventional wisdom, the actions of crowds, and staying on the beaten path.

Ritter, who also teaches a course on financial decision-making, says another reason it's often hard for individuals to make money decisions is because they're not trained to think about things like mortgages, car loans, and investments on a *daily* basis. These topics are largely foreign until we are forced to deal with them. But what about spending? I asked. We certainly do that on a day-to-day basis, but still many times without really thinking about the consequences. "That's a matter of people putting more weight on current gratification versus thinking about the future." As humans, we emotionally prefer to live in the now and deal with tomorrow when it arrives.

My Story: Finding My Financial Persona

In my early 20s, I made more money mistakes than I'm willing to admit. But thanks to my constant exposure to all-things money and access to experts and professionals in every financial field, I was able to reverse those mistakes. This access alone wasn't what gave me the motivation or the drive to stick to a sound financial regimen.

For me, my financial confidence and empowerment was an emotional and psychological journey more than anything else. I discovered that you can learn all you can about the do's and don'ts of money management, but unless you have the mindset and the right behaviors in place, it's very hard to make intelligent moves. What were the emotions I channeled to help me find this strength?

First, I felt obligated *to be a financial do-gooder. I believed that if I was put in a position to offer people savings advice, I, for one, should not be in debt.*

I also knew I had no excuse but to make healthy choices with my money. Looking back at how my parents, who journeyed to the United States with two suitcases and very little money, managed to build their finances and create a comfortable life for their family, I really had no justification *for getting into financial difficulty.*

I assumed control *of the situation. I was also, frankly, a bit afraid of the consequences of* not *getting my act together. I knew that my parents wouldn't bail me out if I ended up over my head in credit card debt. (More on the benefits of scaring yourself straight in order to take control of your money in a later chapter.)*

And I felt a little obsessed with my money, wanting to make sure I never lived beyond my means.

Finally, I recognized I had milestones and goals *to achieve, and therefore I had the desire to become financially fit. I remember graduating from college and driving away from Penn State thinking, "My life starts now. No more waiting for when I 'grow up,'" and with that came immediate financial responsibilities. With everything having a price tag in life, I knew the earlier I started thinking and saving toward my goals, the more likely I could achieve them. Once I crossed that emotional and mental bridge, I was then able to execute on what I knew were sound financial methods. I never let go of these forceful emotions.*

Searching for answers as to why personal finance is so difficult to digest, so tough to triumph, has been a preoccupation and intellectual pursuit of mine for several years. I realized early on in my profession that while there is no end to financial literature and material for older Americans like our parents and grandparents, young adults are severely underserved. There is little that addresses and guides college students and young professionals toward a secure financial life. Yet, as a group, we have no shortage of financial struggles. On average we are saddled with student loans and credit card debt, fight to find well-paying work, and have little to no health insurance.

Then a couple years ago, the economy went into a fetal position. We slid into a recession, and many of us felt we had gone back to the drawing board. We didn't just lose money. We lost our bearings. Many of the goals we had identified, chased after, and hoped for vanished. For me, it was an extremely busy time, fulfilling editorial assignments, answering people's questions on- and offline, and going on TV to break down the stock market crash and the housing debacle and to offer shreds of positive news in this wretched economic environment. I interviewed economists, fund advisors, investors, entrepreneurs, cab drivers, therapists, and, most important, everyday Americans for their insight into where we went wrong, what they wish they'd known, and their hopes for the future.

Sure enough, consumers could tell you exactly where they went wrong. They hadn't paid enough attention to the "signs," they trusted the wrong people, they didn't work hard enough, they got scammed, they were lied to, they had too much optimism, and so forth. But why bother with the past? Putting the pieces back together was the main issue at task now for most people—and for many young adults, this was just the beginning.

To get back on track, you need to understand the behavioral and disciplinary commitments needed to build a financial foundation based on reason and personal aspirations. It's not so much about definitions or calculators. You're wondering how to move into a more elevated world of managing your money to bring security for today and the rest of your life. It is about money, but it's more about *you*.

My Story: Lessons from Reality

I was recently able to test this thinking on SOAPnet's Bank of Mom & Dad. In 2009, I was intimately involved in this pioneering television series that revealed the financial skeletons in the participants' closets, making them come face to face with their financial hardships, their debt, and overspending. It was a far cry from the top-rated reality shows big networks backed season after season, like American Idol *or* The Biggest Loser. *It was a risky show, not exactly escapist television. This was in-your-face, real-life drama about the one thing we, as a society, have yet to openly and wholeheartedly discuss: our money conflicts.*

My task each week was to provide the participants— women in their late 20s and early 30s—with solid advice that we hoped would give them the necessary tools to resolve their financial messes. In return, I received an education as to some of the reasons we, as a society and particularly women, overspend and compile debt. In many cases, these women were highly educated, came from supporting families, and made above-average salaries. So why were they $20,000, $30,000, $60,000 in debt? It was not because they failed to understand the slippery slope of credit card usage, that spending $1,000 on boots was beyond their means, or that their daily $4 Starbucks latte destroyed their ability to save for a rainy day. The problem ran much deeper than that. To get to the root of the issue, I needed to take money out of the equation, at least at first. Instead of beginning our meetings with lengthy sermons about sound money management, I dug into their childhood a bit, into their personal relationships, their goals, and what in life made them happy. I had to know, where's your head at? What do you want? Where do you see yourself in five years? What would Dr. Phil ask?

I really got under people's skin for the first time in my career as I tried to open the emotional and mental floodgates and encourage these individuals to face their fears, weaknesses, and dependencies. My theory was if I could get them to care about their lives and their personal goals first, then suddenly making the right financial choices would not be so difficult or so detestable a task. And I was proved right.

The emotional baggage on Bank of Mom & Dad ran the gamut—from poor self-esteem to strained personal relationships, dependency on others, and a reluctance to just "grow up."

For some women, their money (or borrowed money, as it usually was) had become a substance that they abused to make themselves feel better and live their ideal life (or what they perceived to be ideal).

Shameeka, a 29-year-old nurse from Brooklyn, New York, came on the show, desperate to rein in her $60,000 of debt and begin a new chapter in her life that included *marriage and family. Granted, most people may not be in as dire straights as Shameeka. (In fact, viewers would write in to me, relieved to know that their financial mess wasn't as bad as the women on* Bank of Mom & Dad.*) That said, the show had significant takeaways for people experiencing difficult financial circumstances. Money aside, many viewers could still relate to Shameeka. She was the girl next door, a hardworking nurse with a beautiful smile. She was your friend who always dressed perfectly and gave the best restaurant recommendations. But beneath the Louis Vuitton handbag and Tory Burch flats, Shameeka was an emotional mess who used money like a pill. Spending money made her feel better, but only for a short while, just until her underlying pain resurfaced. She knew enough to realize there was a better life out there for her but didn't know how to cross that bridge and start building her financial life. She just wanted to be happy.*

As was usually the case with the participants on Bank of Mom & Dad, *their drama was never over the money. Their behavioral issues with money stemmed from deep-rooted emotional struggles. Shameeka, for example, had an extremely strained relationship with her mom. Just as much as she wanted to be debt free and have a clean financial start, she wanted to develop a closer bond with her mother. In our first meeting, she confessed that she wished she had a healthier relationship with her mom and that until that was achieved, she couldn't imagine getting out of her rut. She filled the void in her heart by filling her closet with high-end clothes and shoes and by taking expensive vacations. Her bond with her mom was cordial at best, volatile at worst. Some background: Mom had Shameeka when she was just a teenager, and it was decided that Shameeka's grandmother would assume the role of Shameeka's primary caretaker. As a result, that mother-daughter bond never quite formed, and now almost 30 years later, Shameeka desperately longed for a deeper connection with her young mother. But the two often failed to see eye to eye, and knowing Shameeka's money troubles, her mom was openly critical, which didn't do much to help her daughter's confidence.*

Their relationship continues to be a work in progress. But after coming to terms with the ultimate root of her financial mismanagement, confronting her mom, and getting her feelings out on the table, Shameeka felt a huge weight lifted and was compelled to finally change her behavior and begin building a foundation for a secure financial life, with or without her mom's companionship. Her mom didn't quite give her the support she was hoping for, and although Shameeka felt lonely, she somehow found it within herself to commit to change, to dedicate herself to her future, and to ignore the hurt feelings stemming from her past. Shameeka accepted that she is the only one responsible for her actions and must therefore face reality on her own.

Be Money Smart

Being money smart is not just about knowing definitions to financial
terms and calculating compound interest with a calculator. It's not
enough to simply pay your bills on time, clip coupons, and subscribe
to *The Wall Street Journal*. Being money smart requires willpower, a
confident spirit, intuition, a commitment to your personal and professional goals, and sometimes a little thinking outside the box.

Your journey awaits!

Part I

Draft Your Financial Blueprint

1 — Personalize *Rich*

"Rich is some sh°t you could lose with a crazy summer and a drug habit."

Chris Rock, comedian

My first recollection of the term *rich* dates back to around Halloween 1984. While my other 4-year-old friends dressed up as ghosts, witches, and Snow White, my costume was Richie Rich, "The richest kid in the world."

Hanna-Barbera's Richie Rich was a cartoon series about a fictitious little boy whose animated life couldn't have been further from my childhood truth. Whereas this young boy summered on a gold-painted yacht, I elbowed my way around the sandpit at Elm Park in Worcester, Massachusetts. Richie had a butler and a maid, as well as a room full of stuffed animals, video game machines, an outdoor tennis court, and shiny blonde hair. I did not have such luxuries. From this show's viewpoint, rich meant having lots of stuff, countless dollar bills, and a smile locked on your face.

Fortunately, my education of what constitutes rich didn't end there, but it was a memorable influence. For many of us, our initial introduction to *rich* goes back to childhood and usually focuses on the material aspects. This is not only an incomplete picture; it doesn't quite speak to personal needs and goals. What about the kind of rich that leads to personal gratification?

Rich: Up Close and Personal

How you perceive your own wealth is really a function of behavioral leanings, life experience, and, most important, personal philosophy. I contend that to be rich, you should also feel fulfilled. Interestingly enough, many individuals whom the government would classify as rich (at an annual salary of $250,000 and higher) think of themselves as quite the opposite: bereft of happiness and satisfaction. A study published in the *Journal of Research in Personality* reported that recent college graduates earning more money than their fellow grads of equal standing had greater systems of depression than their peers.[1] Even more surprising, a highly referenced study about the correlation between lottery winners and accident victims found that there was no difference between the happiness level of 22 lottery winners and comparison samples of average people or paraplegics.[2] The takeaway here is that money doesn't lead to happiness or fulfillment—being rich and feeling richly fulfilled are two separate concepts. The *Journal of Research in Personality* study went on to hypothesize that the reason financially rich people don't have better attitudes on life is because they're too narrow-minded. They focus on the goals of being materially rich as opposed to the deeper values and goals in life such as committed relationships, having a family, leading a healthful life, making plans for your future, and working in a job you love.

Although wealth doesn't correlate with happiness, it helps maintain one's lifestyle and drive future opportunities. Harvard professor David Gilbert and the author of *Stumbling on Happiness* wrote in his book that "wealth increases human happiness when it lifts people out of abject poverty and into the middle class...but it does little to increase happiness thereafter." So, it's true that a level of happiness does come with the ability to afford basic needs. Beyond that, however, happiness evolves from the quality of your personal, professional, and financial relationships.

Rich *as used in the title of this book is not about chasing a
dollar figure or accumulating more and more wealth—
that's not the end game.*

Rich: A Paradigm Shift

In the thick of the recession, I called up my friend and economist
Joseph Brusuelas to get his take on this and to see whether, in fact,
the rich were changing their ways. Joe theorized that the negative
impact on the wealthy during the recession may have triggered a
long-term cultural shift that has changed how the rest of the country
spends and values wealth.

Wealth in this country became not just about accumulation. In
early 2010, Sallie Krawcheck, the head of Bank of America's global
wealth and investment management division and one of *Forbes* magazine's "most powerful women," explained a paradigm shift among
the bank's clientele on CNBC. Based on the bank's newest survey
results,[3] the wealthy in this country are less concerned with accumulating a certain *amount* of wealth for retirement. Instead, these
investors are searching for a certain quality of life and a way to make
the most of their time. "People are cutting back on luxuries to spend
more time with their families," said Sallie.

We're seeing the new definition of rich playing out at all tiers of
society; it is punctuated by security, savings, enjoying life, and an
emphasis on value and quality over quantity.

Your Formula for Rich

So, given the aftermath of the recession, the Fed figures, and the
Richie Rich lifestyle, what's rich *to you*? What does being *and* feeling
rich, together at the same time, constitute? What is being *holistically*

rich? Let's focus on the emotions that will be foundation of your formula. For starters, feeling rich is mainly about feeling *secure*. So, let me ask you: What does security mean in your life? Is it knowing that you're doing all you can in your power to protect your health, house, income, savings, investments, and the security of your loved ones? How about having money to donate and to be generous to others? Is rich being secure at work and in your career?

Maybe you can't buy everything you want right now without comparing price tags and cutting coupons, but you sure *feel* rich because you know you have a firm financial foundation that's working for you today and in the future. Feeling rich is a better goal, in my mind, and a far more achievable ideal than actually being *numerically* rich. Rich is, in addition to security, the quality and value of our possessions, friends and relationships.

Getting Started: Covering All Bases

Covering your financial bases means you are prepared for the unexpected (job loss, surprise baby number two, a broken dishwasher) as well as the expected (annual doctor visits, your mortgage, your retirement). Your bases may not get covered all at once, but hitting these marks early on will enable you to build a foundation for a comfortable financial life. Here's a summary of the ten most critical bases you need to secure to achieve peace of mind, gain control over your money, and keep your lifestyle in check:

1. **Sufficient earnings.** You need to make money. How much? At the bare minimum, enough to cover your necessities from food to housing, transportation, heat, clothing, and medical insurance. If you want a child, you'll need to boost your earnings or retire from dining out and shopping. Like my childhood friend Targol, who just became a new mom, tells me, "Babies cost a fortune—not only do you need to spend a lot of money for diapers, healthcare, clothes, and such, but now you have someone

else's future to save for." Babycenter.com estimates the average first-year baby costs at more than $10,000. To cope, Targol and her husband John have a separate savings account for baby Cameron's expenses, in addition to starting a college savings fund. That's what's known as *milestone savings* (explained later in this list).

2. **Savings.** The recession has turned us back into savers. In 2006—when life was merry and people's homes were appreciating 25% a quarter—the savings rate was a fat 0%. Today, after the threat of not being able to make ends meet or losing a job, the savings rate has reversed to a near a 15-year high of around 5%. Targol and John (the new parents) have about six months of savings resting in a liquid account. John was briefly unemployed before Cameron's arrival, and that was enough to make rainy-day savings a priority. A simple way of structuring your savings is to automatically deduct a portion of your biweekly or monthly paycheck into an account. Using your earnings, allocate a weekly or monthly amount to a liquid (i.e., readily converted into cash) savings account. Do so until you have at least six months to nine months of savings tucked away in case of an unexpected setback like a job loss. Bear in mind that during this recession it is taking the unemployed roughly 30 weeks to find a new job, and sometimes it isn't an equal or higher paying one. Having said that, research shows we hate seeing our paychecks shrink. A small trick to motivate yourself to save is to, as Richard Thaler and Cass Sustein, behavioral experts and authors of the best-seller *Nudge*, state, "Save More Tomorrow." Their theory is that if you precommit to saving a portion of a future salary hike toward retirement or rainy-day savings, you'll save more over time and feel less pain doing so. If you expect you'll get a $5,000 raise, precommit to saving half of that. Or, the next time you get an unexpected cash bonus or surprise lump sum of money, commit to putting at least half of it into a savings account right away.

3. **Retirement savings.** 401k plans and individual retirement accounts (IRAs) dominate the world of retirement savings tools. Like rainy-day savings, automatically investing a fraction of your earnings into these accounts helps add to your financial security. Remember that the younger you are, the more aggressive you want to be. In my 20s, I put about 10% of my income toward my 401k and mostly in stock funds. In addition, I max out my IRA contribution allowance every year. Now that I'm self-employed and no longer have access to a 401k, I've set up a SEP IRA, which is a type of IRA strictly for the self-employed and small business owners that lets you be more aggressive than a traditional IRA. With a SEP, I can tuck away up to $49,000 a year (if I could). With a traditional IRA, I'm limited to $5,000 a year.

4. **Milestone savings.** What's on your wish list in the next five years? Hoping to buy a house? Get married? Start a family? Build a business? Send a child to private school? It's going to cost you, but it won't be as daunting if you start socking away money in advance. Even if you're not certain you'll hit these milestones in five years, ten years, or ever, it's smart to have goals and look forward to your future. At the least, your goals will motivate you to get out of bed in the morning.

5. **Debt elimination.** Rich people don't have debt. They may have credit cards and use them to score points, but they certainly don't carry balances beyond 30 days. They pay in full each month. You can't afford a fulfilling life with debt on your personal balance sheet.

6. **Sufficient insurance.** From health to disability to home and life, you're not secure unless you have proper insurance. Although the healthcare situation in the United States is in transition, this shouldn't deter you from putting some of your income toward a simple health insurance plan that will cover

the basics like doctor checkups, prescriptions, and x-rays. And why is disability insurance important? If you become disabled and a doctor says you can't work in your profession (or any job for that matter) and you don't have proper disability insurance, you won't be able to continue collecting a paycheck from your employer. And being disabled doesn't just mean breaking your arms. It can also mean a psychological or emotional condition that prevents you from working. According to the Insurance Information Institute (III), at age 35, people have a 45% chance of being disabled for 90 days or longer before their sixty-fifth birthday. And among those people, there's a 70% chance of being disabled for another two years.

7. **Home equity.** If you don't own a home, you can skip to the next base, although I encourage you to consider buying a home if you plan to work and live somewhere for more than five years. Is your house really an asset? Or a liability? Home equity has helped make a lot of people wealthy and simultaneously many people very poor over the past five years. You could earn $200,000 a year and have several of these bases covered, but if your mortgage is greater than the current market value of your house—with no appreciation in sight and a rate that's set to adjust higher in the next year or two—your net worth may be approaching a loss. To cover this base, you need to find ways to end up house *rich* at the end of the month rather than house *poor*—actions like refinancing, renting out the basement, and investing in smart home upgrades that will offer a positive return on investment. (We also explore walking away from your mortgage in Chapter 4, "Embrace Your Relationship with Money.") No doubt you'll have better years than others, as housing prices fluctuate, but if you consistently pay down your principal, history shows you should be in the black in the long run, primed to cash out when time comes to sell.

8. **Defined financial responsibilities in your relationship.** Who's in charge of the bills? How do you decide on big purchases? Do you have a separate savings account and a joint savings account (you should)? Having open communication in your relationship as it pertains to your financial obligations and goals is one base you can't afford not to cover. In their marriage, Targol takes care of the finances. They're both numbers people, both have MBAs, but they find it's easier to allocate the day-to-day responsibilities to one person. Occasionally, they may switch off to give the other person some familiarity with how the gas and heat get paid, but the couple has defined their responsibilities, and that adds to their security, a big rich factor. "Our system is that I am in control of our finances," says Targol. "The budgeting, saving, bill paying, planning, etc. Of course, I consult him when needed, but we've mutually decided that I'm just 'better at it,' I have more time to do it and, frankly, more interest in controlling it!" (Targol is a self-described Type A control freak.)

9. **Money that *works*.** When asked what defines being rich, many of the respondents in a survey I took answered "having your money work for you so that you can pursue what you love and not be stressed." Of course, this base can get covered only when you have enough money to put to work, which is why it's covered later in this list. At some point, once all other bases are covered, you should start to be more aggressive in getting your money to work for you. Now, technically, putting money in a traditional savings account or certificate of deposit is "working" for you. It's yielding, at last check, anywhere from 1% to 2%. But that's not really what I'm getting at here. Good work is when money earns you annual average returns of more than 5%, 6%, 7%, and higher from working in stocks and mutual funds. *Great* work is when you put your money in *alternative* (albeit riskier) investments that may possibly yield even higher

returns (for example, real estate, a business plan, and let's not forget, you). Investing in yourself to advance your skills is one of the greatest ways to put your money to work, something we delve into later in this book.

10. **Charitable giving.** Social psychologists conducted a study in 2005 and found spending on others, being charitable and philanthropic, boosts happiness.[4] The survey tested college students' happiness levels before and after an experiment in which half the participants were given money to spend on themselves and the other half of the participants were given money to spend on others (for example, a charitable contribution). In the end, those who spent money on others admitted to having a greater level of happiness. But beyond the selfish pleasure that follows charitable giving, it's important to give back because it's good karma and it makes you appreciate and be thankful for what you have. My mom always said one of the keys to a satisfied life was not to keep your head in the skies but to be mindful of the less fortunate. Having an awareness of what you have and what others have *not* keeps you grounded, appreciative, and respectful. It reminds you to embrace all that is good and positive in your life, your riches.

---

[1] C. P. Niemiec, R. M. Ryan, and E. L. Deci, "The Path Taken: Consequences of Attaining Intrinsic and Extrinsic Aspirations in Post-College Life," *Journal of Research in Personality*, 2009.

[2] Philip Brickman, Dan Coates, and Ronnie Janoff-Bulman, "Lottery Winners and Accident Victims: Is Happiness Relative?" *Journal of Personality and Social Psychology* 36(8), 1978.

[3] *Merrill Lynch Quarterly Affluent Insight Survey*, January 2010.

[4] Elizabeth Dunn, Lara Aknin, and Micahel Norton. "Spending Money on Others Promotes Happiness," University of British Columbia, Harvard Business School, 2005.

2

Establish Goals

"The quest for money is a misguided goal."
Joseph J. Luciani, *The Power of Self-Coaching*

Let me tell you about a young woman who came to me for financial help last year. She was 24, mostly unemployed—except for a few one-off promotional jobs here and there—and living with her boyfriend rent free. She had some $20,000 in debt, was struggling to make ends meet, and had come to New York City to pursue modeling and acting. "What are your goals," I asked at our first meeting. "To be a famous actress and make millions of dollars," she said, with an innocent sparkle in her eye. She would refuse to listen to her naysaying mom and friends who explained she had a one-in-a-billion chance of becoming the next Angelina Jolie. You need to find an alternative career path, they pleaded with her. But the young woman refused to focus on anything else. For that, I guess you have to give her some kudos for being strong willed and adamant about her goals. But, really, what about a backup plan? Or let's say she does become the next Hollywood starlet. What happens if and when she strikes it rich? After all, just because you have money and fame doesn't mean you'll know how to manage it. This is someone who racked up $20,000 in debt. What's to say she's not going to fall into the debt trap again? What's going to keep her from falling off the millionaire wagon? Or, let's be fair, what if she never gets on the wagon to begin with?

The goal to have boatloads of cash—but not having a plan or roadmap to protect said money—is something I wouldn't wish on my worst enemy. It's practically a curse. Think of the people in this country who are linked to giant sums of money upfront, such as professional athletes, lottery winners, and celebrities, and you'll see that these rich folks are quite prone to financial ruin. Reports show one-third of lotto winners file for bankruptcy within the first five years after their win.[1] Four out of five professional football players in the NFL go bankrupt within two years of retirement.[2] And celebs have their own share of woes. In 2009, the IRS reportedly filed a multi-million-dollar tax lien against actor Nick Cage.[3] And New York socialite Veronica Hearst faced foreclosure on her $45-million Florida residence that same year.[4]

So let's forget about money for the next few pages. I find that when we focus on our utmost desires, our dreams and aspirations first, we elegantly find our way back to the topic of money in a positive and accepting way. Having goals and pursuing them almost inevitably means having a firm grip on your money. The idea of starting a family, building a house, or planning a wedding can motivate us to be financially responsible. But thinking about saving when you don't really know what you're saving for can seem pointless and uninspiring.

Goals keep the rest of your financial life in order. When you desire to have a house and you make this dream a constant thought in your day-to-day life, when you think about furnishing the house, living in the house, raising your family in the house, growing old in the house and the memories you will create there, the house becomes a sought-after passion and encourages you to follow your course in life in a healthy path toward the finish line. Along the way, you don't overspend on frivolous things, you start saving well and consciously for a down payment, you research interest rates, you explore neighborhoods, and you spend time talking to realtors and on other activities that support this goal, as opposed to spending time and money on other things that distract you from buying the house of your dreams.

This is not to say that all the wealthy folks mentioned at the beginning of the chapter (the athletes, the celebs) fell into financial difficulties because they did not have goals or ambitions. I'm absolutely certain they did or else they wouldn't have become so successful in their careers. As they built and sustained their careers, they somehow became misguided, and that negatively affected their financial situations. Some might have gotten carried away with the trappings of success, whereas others entrusted their money to the wrong people. Others just overlooked the fact that their money wouldn't last forever. As for the lottery winners? They, too, may have had great goals at one point, but their sudden encounter with vast sums of money made them lose their grip on reality and forget what was really important.

The more certain and specific our goals are,
the better able we are to be productive, stay the course,
and sniff out trouble.

An important reason why goals are so vital in life is that they help us to commit to the hierarchy of our personal needs and wants. With defined ambitions, we suddenly don't need or want many things that we previously may have coveted. The phrase *having it all* doesn't literally mean having every material thing in the universe. It means having what you need and some things that you want and overall feeling very pleased and content with your life and your relationships in the long run. You've heard it before—it's about quality, not quantity.

Finally, goals help define and shape our lives and give us something to work toward. Whatever your goals—whether it's to live as healthy a life as possible, to earn a black belt in karate, be the "perfect" parent, start your own clothing company, buy a home, buy a second home, or to travel the country on your motorbike—you must realize that all goals carry price tags, both emotional and financial. Similarly, all goals have tradeoffs. If you want to upgrade to a larger home in the next two years, you might need to shore up a down payment, and doing so might require living on less for some time. The key is to keep those price tags and tradeoffs in mind while mainly focusing on the *behavioral* changes you need to make to achieve your goals.

Goal Ambivalence

Fighting goal ambivalence is the longest and trickiest part of the process, but once you defeat it, there should be few barriers between you and the accomplishment of your goals. To be clear, *goal ambivalence* refers to those who don't care enough to or have any clues about identifying what's important to them and where they want to be in the next three months, let alone the next three, five, ten years of life.

On my television program, *The Bank of Mom & Dad*, I worked with Stacey, a 23-year-old part-time preschool teacher who had yet to finish college. She'd been in and out of school since graduating from high school, uncertain about the direction she wanted to take (despite the fact that her parents were willing to pay for her education). Frankly, I don't think her future was a serious consideration for her at that time. She was living for the moment, teaching by day, shopping by afternoon, and hanging out with friends by night. She spent all that she made on day-to-day expenses, with none going toward savings. She had also managed to rack up a considerable amount of credit card debt along the way.

Stacey's story raises these questions: At what point do you need to start getting serious? How do you get over financial indifference and become committed to change?

Ask yourself these questions:

- What's keeping you from getting off your seat?
- Do you know what your reality is and that there's a better reality waiting for you if only you identify it and make a plan to work toward it?
- Why don't you desire to hit certain milestones?

- Do you feel that life is unpredictable and perhaps that uncertainty is making you feel out of control of your life?
- Do you know what makes you happy?
- Are you trapped by your debt and don't think you can focus on your future yet?
- Are you financially dependent on someone else, and is that dependence keeping you from charting your own course?

These are all valid questions, and the resulting emotions can cause goal ambivalence, but at some point you need to assume responsibility and make plans for your life.

For Stacey, a significant part of her goal ambivalence was that she didn't need to have a grasp on her reality. She didn't know what it was like in the real world. After all, she lived in a nurturing bubble where her parents and friends seemed to always be around to bail her out or support her when times got financially rough. She had no inspiring role models and no real understanding of how a college degree can boost earnings potential. (Average annual earnings for a high school graduate are about $30,000 a year, whereas those with a Bachelor's degree earn on average $50,000 a year [based on census data].)

To snap Stacey out of this, her parents and I had her volunteer to help others who were less fortunate. To really overcome her goal ambivalence, she needed to understand not only her reality but an alternate reality, one of near-poverty and one where family doesn't exist. We sent her to a local soup kitchen to meet with older adults who had had financial setbacks and who had no family or close friends to give them a helping hand. That experience helped her realize how fortunate she was and how she was taking her family for granted. She saw how necessary it is to be able to stand on your own two feet and why it's helpful to set goals for yourself. In addition, we used a bit of a scare tactic. We forced Stacey to confront her grandmother, who had cosigned on a car loan for Stacey that had become delinquent. Their relationship had been greatly strained as a result of Stacey's financial negligence. Apologizing and hearing directly from her grandma how her behavior had ruined her credit, as well as her trust in her, was an enormous wakeup call for Stacey.

Taking personal responsibility and having goals (even if she doesn't map out every last detail of what she wants to do in life) will help motivate Stacey out of a state of laziness and unaccountability, where she's been for most her young adult life. The first sign that you've conquered goal ambivalence is that you feel mobilized and ready to make a plan. Today, Stacey is back in school and has managed to find a place of her own. The next goal? To find a full-time job after college and pay down her debt.

Mastering Goal Ambivalence

So, how can you defeat goal ambivalence? First, you need to do some homework and soul searching. Translation: You need to stop whatever you're doing and take a time out—anywhere from an hour to a long weekend away—to analyze the direction your life is headed and your feelings about that. Bring a journal, bring music, go down memory lane to when you were a child, and think about what your goals were back then. Your instincts are very good when you're a kid because your thoughts and perceptions have yet to be muddied. As a kid, you think simply and innocently. So, if you remember wanting to be a fireman when you were just 8 years old, there may actually be some truth to that. Perhaps your true calling is not to be a firefighter per se, but perhaps a problem solver and humanitarian.

In addition to your journals, your iPod, and childhood memories, find a mentor, talk to friends and family, and talk to people who've been in your shoes and have struggled with the concept of happiness and wealth. Who are your happiest and most balanced friends? Give them a call and grab some coffee.

My Story:
Soul Searching

In 2005, I went to the Bahamas (on a budget) with my best friend Kate. It was my first serious vacation as an independent adult. The timing was good because I was feeling pretty rundown at work and was sort of going through a quarter-life crisis (being about 26 years old at the time). I was asking myself introspective questions, such as: Where is my life headed? What makes me happy? Will I ever make enough money to really save? I hustled my way through the corporate world and was still trying to figure out my Zen place.

My inspiration for getting out of the rut was the fact that I wanted to really amp up my career and earn more money. I felt I'd hit a wall at work and wanted to be more excited about my job. I also wanted to start saving and investing aggressively. During my soul searching, I remembered thinking how I didn't really have much of an excuse to not push harder since that's what my parents always did to provide a great life for us and they had far less than I did at my age. My parents also taught me that little in life is ever handed to you. If you want something badly, you need to go grab it yourself. Holding onto that lesson, I quickly started networking when I got back to New York. Within a month I had landed a new job. I also began a personal project—outside of my 9 to 5— drafting a book proposal about how to make the most of your financial life in your 20s. Two years later, You're So Money *hit bookstore shelves and marked a turning point in my career and personal life.*

Finally, you have to commit to your goals: mind, body, and soul. Imagine what life will be like. How will you feel? The goal has to come out of your head and permeate your senses, travel to your heart and your being. It's known as *visualization*, something humans are inherently good at. According to Dan Ariely, author of *Predictably Irrational* and the James B. Duke Professor of Behavioral Economics at Duke University, "We do more vision more hours of the day than we do anything else…and we're good at it." "What's more," says Ariely, "when it comes to visual illusions, we can see the mistakes." Visualization will enable your whole body and brain to understand how this accomplishment may (or may not) resonate in your life. Even professional athletes, who often deal with extreme pressure and sometimes suffer a great deal of anxiety, use visualization to control and perhaps enhance their performance.

Of course, you don't need to go to the Bahamas to triumph over goal ambivalence or indecisiveness (although the sandy beaches and crystal-clear waters are a nice touch). I could have easily gotten revved up after a weekend at home, running, reading, and talking through my concerns with family and close friends. Everyone has his or her own process. The important thing is that you acknowledge you want and need to move forward and accomplish your goals and that you're willing to work hard and do what it takes to achieve those goals. Don't get overwhelmed, either. The objective is to create a viable goal that you can focus on and accomplish in the near term. If you can set goals that apply from now through eternity, go for it, with the understanding that you can change your mind as life goes on. For now, though, based on where you are today and where you want to be in, say, five years, what are your goals? To answer this, you must come to understand the type of person you are, the kind of life you want, and try to focus on the positive (while being realistic).

Finding Your Will and Your Way

You won't beat goal ambivalence by pulling goals out of thin air or leaving them open ended. The spirit or the will is necessary to have, but what about the way? What about the strategy and the follow through? Here are seven steps to help establish your willpower and follow through:

> **Step 1: Own up to your obligations.** What do you absolutely, unequivocally need to address in your life? How must you stay the course in order to accomplish goals? An obligation is different from a goal. An obligation is something that you need to do to survive, plain and simple. Often, people chase their goals while forgetting or not recognizing their obligations, like earning money, paying rent, paying your bills, and if you have a family, providing and caring for them. Chasing a dream without assuming responsibility for your obligations is like buying the car of your dreams and not having the means to pay down the loan. Or still another example: Getting in your car and driving out West to find a job in Hollywood while ditching your lease back on the East Coast. When you think of what your obligations are, think of what you are *required* to do: legally, financially, and morally. In some cases, your obligations are plain and simple. For example, make enough money to pay your rent on time. In others, your obligations are very personal. For instance, devote time to your ailing parents who could use your assistance. Jonas, a 34-year-old marketing consultant from New York, says his obligations are providing for his family, protecting his home, saving for retirement, growing his career, and of course, enjoying life. (Yes, enjoying life should be a requirement.) Knowing his obligations has helped Jonas better manage his money and his goals, which include adding two more kids to the family. "I find myself managing my money a lot more conservatively than I have in the past," Jonas said. "I'm

also questioning myself on purchases and trying to understand my current needs over my wants."

Step 2: Identify opportunities. Part of recognizing your goals and understanding how you can accomplish them involves identifying the opportunities that surround you. You may have an idea for a business and a friend who's interested in the same thing. This might be your opportunity to collaborate and get your goals off the ground. You might live close to a university and have been thinking about going back to school. There's a potential opportunity to get that elevated degree you always wanted and get a raise at work. You may have an idea for a book and have a friend who can refer you to a literary agent. That's one big opportunity to bounce your ideas off a professional and market your idea to different publishers. Or how about this: The country's in the midst of a recession, and you want to take advantage of markdowns and make a smart bet. Keeping your eyes and ears open during a financial crisis is a great way to seize opportunities. In 2008, my friend Lydia and her husband Rick did what few Americans dared to do at that time. When the news was all about foreclosure and falling home values, the couple decided to seize the moment and scoop up a second home to serve as their family's vacation spot. In that year, the number of people purchasing a second home—either a vacation home or an investment property to rent out—dropped by 30% from 2007, based on recent data from the National Association of Realtors.[5] In the meantime, the median price of a vacation home fell 23% in 2008, from $195,000 to $150,000. It was always a goal of theirs to have a home away from home, and with more inventory and fallen prices, they figured it was a smart time to make the move. In the end, they believe they saved 20% off the 2007 market price. "It seemed like the perfect time to invest," said Lydia, who hopes their new investment will, over time, offset the recent losses in their retirement portfolios.

I like to use the Web for inspiration. When I was a sophomore in college interning at an online media firm in New York City, I, like most interns, had some free time on my hands. Curious to identify my ideal job, I began looking up people I admired on the Internet, from various accomplished journalists, to authors, television hosts, and producers. I examined their biographies to see what opportunities they grasped and how I might be able to replicate them in some way myself. I learned about the advantages they had via higher education, through living in New York City, via working in challenging environments, and through being entrepreneurial. Sometimes—for these men and women—opportunities arose while being at the right place at the right time. But, they were there *and* aware enough to seize the opportunities, weren't they? It was an inspiring exercise then and one that I still do from time to time when I am considering the next steps in my career and personal life.

Step 3: Analyze price tags. All of your goals, whether personal or professional, have a financial denominator. Everything in life has a price tag, a cost more or less. If one of your goals is to build a house in the next three years, you have to consider the cost of the land, the architect, and building materials. Also, what expenses may have to take a backseat while you save up and pay for this house? What changes are you willing to make to fit these goals into your life's picture? The same goes for starting a family.

While there's never a perfect time to have kids, according to my friend Michael who has five children under the age of 12, there are ways to be financially prepared for the arrival of a new life, and it starts by understanding all the costs that go into having a child (at least for the first year), including examinations, formula, diapers, clothing, and childcare. Your life will change— for the better, I hope—when you have a family, especially your financial life. It's interesting to hear my expecting friends say things like "this will be my last big clothing purchase for myself before my baby arrives." Meaning, once the baby enters the picture, the family's financial focus turns to the baby and providing for him or her. For some, having a baby means that the days of splurging on Prada are temporarily over. And it's totally worth it.

Step 4: Get specific and aim high. So, now you know what your goals are. Where to next? Well, how specific are your goals? How detail oriented are they? In other words, do you describe one of your goals as "go back to school" or as "go back to school for a Master's degree in sociology, a school located close enough to work so that I can still work part time and study part time?" Is your goal to "buy a home in two years" or "buy a five-bedroom home within a ten-mile radius of our current location, with the goal of putting down 25% in two years."

The more specific your goals, the better you can narrow them down and start working toward them. Knowing you need a 25% down payment may mean you have to adjust your saving strategy. And, obviously, you can only get so specific because some things are simply not up to you. Not everything's a guarantee, no matter how much you plan, set goals, and follow the course. You might want to further your education at a particular school, but doing so will depend on the admissions board. However, knowing in advance the required qualifications, you can try your best to meet the board's expectations and along the way shoot high enough that admission to your second- and third-choice schools become slam dunks. And while you have your heart set out on a colonial-style home, the inventory may be limited in your desired neighborhoods. But knowing you want a five-bedroom home of some sort will encourage you to save more aggressively than you might otherwise for a smaller-sized property, even if it's not in your first-choice design. Always aim high, I guess, is the moral of that story.

Step 5: Raise your goal karma. Now that you understand your obligations, your goals, and their price tags, design a path that will help you track your savings and keep your goals in check. This roadmap should be filled with your obligations and your goals first. Along the way, you may find room for extra fillers (such as dinners out, a new wardrobe, a new bike). As long as you keep your eye on your obligations and your goals, you shouldn't fall off track. As part of your roadmap, it's critical that you take along one or a few buddies. A buddy system is where you share your goals with a close friend or relative and use each other's guidance and support as motivation to stay the course. I joke (although it's kind of true) that I insist on calling my mom and getting her opinion on financial things because, for me, it's one way to make sure I don't screw up and buy something frivolous. My mom, I know, will tell me like it is. She wants only the best for me, too, so I know her advice is coming from a good and loving place.

Step 6: Constantly motivate. The New Year is typically a time for people to reexamine their goals and identify what they would like to accomplish or change. But once a year is not enough to really motivate yourself and follow through on your goals. Like a promise to quit smoking or to lose ten pounds, if we only check in once a year on that promise, we're less likely to stay on track.

Goal setting and goal achieving should be an ongoing process, and you want to set up a system to check in with yourself and your goals on a regular basis. One way to do this is to make your goals visual and omnipresent. Begin by writing down your goals on paper and on your computer. I have goals written down in my cell phone, believe it or not. Read and review them at least a few times a week when you have downtime. Having my goals in my cell phone allows for easy access when riding on the subway or when I need something to distract myself with. And by the way, it's okay to modify your goals as much as you want. Better to do this throughout the year than once a year. If you wait until that once-a-year checkup, you might "waste" days, weeks, or even months without realizing that your goals have changed from what you initially set out to accomplish.

The next best way to check in with your goals and motivate yourself is to share your goals with people in your life whom you respect and admire. Surround yourself with people who you know will support you in your dreams. Finally, chart your progress. There are several online tools to help us chart and monitor our financial goals. Most banks and credit unions will let you set up separate savings accounts for personal goals. The online banking site SmartyPig.com, in fact, was set up precisely for goal setters. There, you can create a savings account for your goal (a new kitchen, a new car, a wedding) and invite friends and family to donate money to your account. Once you've reached the finish line, you can redeem your cash either on a debit card or on various gift cards or transfer it to another bank account. The site even has a calculator to help you figure out the ballpark estimate of how much you may need to save.

Step 7: Diversify your goals. Our goals fall into primarily two key areas of life. One the one hand, we have our professional goals, which involve our careers and jobs. On the other, we have personal goals, which are related to health, relationships, and personal development. It's important to have goals in both of these main categories to help fulfill that "richness" in life we explored in the first chapter.

If nothing else, getting in the habit of evaluating your priorities, wishes, and wants is an effective way to make money more tangible and less abstract. By giving your money a purpose, you give your financial life more meaning. In the following chapter, we take this relationship a step further.

[1] *Eagle Tribune*, October 28, 2007.

[2] *Sports Illustrated*, March 23, 2009.

[3] *Detroit News*, July 31, 2009.

[4] Forbes.com, June 3, 2009.

[5] National Association of Realtors, Investment and Vacation Home Buyers Survey, 2009.

3

Craft Your Money Philosophy

"If a man is proud of his wealth, he should not be praised until it is known how he employs it."

Socrates

Everyone has his or her own philosophical theories on various aspects of life, from relationships to staying healthy to work and family—some are more firmly established than others. What are your money philosophies? I agree with Socrates: Your money is practically worthless until you put it to work and have something valuable and honorable to show for it.

Whatever your view, money philosophies are essential because they reemphasize and nourish our goals, in addition to keeping financial obligations in check. They serve as a compass of sorts, helping to guide us through the countless money-related obstacles life presents. In this chapter, I will help you define your financial philosophy and make it a part of your conscious life. Trust that if you can develop a personal money mission statement, it will help lead you to goals, to answers, shed light on what to do with your money, and help you figure out how to make more of it.

The Journey to Creating a Financial Philosophy

Your money philosophy is a basic statement about how you should manage your financial life: how you should save, spend, invest, donate, and control it, in addition to your backup plan should money become tight. This philosophy isn't created in a vacuum. The experiences and behaviors we've previously discussed figure prominently into how financial matters are explicitly or subconsciously managed. It's important to be in tune with these experiences and behaviors because that is often the genesis of our philosophies.

My Story: Unexpected Opportunities

After almost three years working as a correspondent for TheStreet.com, a financial news site, I was laid off along with 20 or so other employees from the already lean-staffed web company in spring 2009. I was stunned and confused, but mostly just sad, especially after my last stop in Jim Cramer's office to thank him for all his support and encouragement over the years. Jim was a co-founder of the company (in addition to being the host of CNBC's Mad Money *and author of numerous books.) Jim was and continues to be a mentor and a friend to me. He generously wrote the foreword and investing section for my first book and later publicly supported it when* You're So Money *was published. He was not involved with the downsizing decisions that spring, he told me, and I believe him.*

On my last day, I expressed my gratitude for his uncon-ditional support. I sort of lost it after our goodbye hug—though, not in front of him. Oh, never.

Instead, I fell into Debbie's arms, his longtime assistant, my waterproof mascara spilling down my cheeks and onto her button-down sweater. Get it together, Torabi, I could hear my high school track coach yelling at me. But I couldn't help it. And at that moment, I felt really, really crappy.

In retrospect, I should have been celebrating my inde-pendence. The night before, I was having an early dinner with my friend John-Paul when I learned of my layoff. John-Paul, a serial entrepreneur, raised his glass and made a toast to my newfound freedom. I knew what he meant and I appreciated it. Still, I was depressed.

To get over this, I needed to change my way of thinking, or maybe it was just that I had to remind myself of my goals, who I was and wanted to be. But that might not have been enough. I needed to also concentrate on my philosophy—the substance behind those goals.

The alternative (feeling sorry for myself and sleeping in until noon) would have been a lot easier. And for the record, yes, I did do that for about five days (maybe six); after all, it was a necessary part of my healing process. You have to allow yourself some time off. But soon you need to take the reins and deal with the situation. You need to psych yourself back into getting out there, find-ing a job, being professionally relevant, and creating a new momentum.

For me, being given a pink slip was a reason to pursue a different career path—working for myself. I had considered leaving the company voluntarily on and off for this purpose, but I don't think I would have done it as early if I hadn't been caught in this particular layoff. It was unpleasant and unplanned, but it was the kick in the pants I needed to take my career to a new level.

The next month I appeared on the NBC Today Show to offer personal finance advice for a segment on careers, during which I talked about how young professionals can bounce back after a layoff, much to the chagrin of others who thought telling six million viewers I was laid off may mean I was not "good enough." Bull. The unemployment rate was creeping toward 10% at the time and amazing, talented, highly qualified workers were in unemployment lines. A layoff was no longer a stigma. I wanted to share my story and wore my unemployment like a badge with honor because with it came a new beginning.

All this to say that my encounter with sudden unemployment, which some of you may relate to, could have easily put me in an indefinite stage of self-doubt, trepidation, and weakness. My goals were put to the test. Could I actually still succeed in my profession as a journalist without a full-time employer? Could I save enough money to buy a house in the next couple of years, as I'd hoped? Could I now still save as aggressively for retirement? I guessed so…but recognizing my goals, alone, didn't seem quite enough to get me out of my quasi-uncertain phase. I needed philosophies for life, money, and career that I could latch onto for reaffirmation.

The upshot? Viewers wrote in to say how much they appreciated my candor on the Today Show *and that it offered them hope that there is life after losing your day job. That year, I won the distinguished Alumni Achievement Award from the Smeal College of Business at Penn State. Addressing the faculty and staff at the ceremony, I said that it's funny how you can be handed a pink slip and be honored for great achievement in the same year.*

Putting Philosophy to the Test

My layoff caused me to address my own beliefs head on. During this time, I became more convinced that the five philosophies that I had put in place years earlier would carry me through this rough patch and keep me on the path toward achieving my goals. I shared these perspectives with Meredith Viera during that same morning I appeared on the *Today Show*:

> **Philosophy 1:** When it comes to your career, you have to be entrepreneurial, stay in charge of your income somehow, sometimes think creatively, and always find value in your experiences to help get you to the next step.

> **Philosophy 2:** I, along with 10% of the U.S. workforce at that time, could now vouch that a full-time job was no guarantee. So, you have to hope for the best and prepare for the worst. If you can't afford your lifestyle while working toward future goals with one job, you need a second or a third.

Philosophy 3: The more you have to do, the more you get done. Having a few jobs kept me busy and helped me stay organized and responsible.

Philosophy 4: Pursue what makes you happy; work hard and trust that the money will somehow follow. After all, I didn't stay up all night filing stories from 2004 to 2008 for *AM New York* on the side because of the $75 per article they gave me (which amounted to less than 15 cents per word). It was because I valued the opportunity and hoped it would lead to bigger things, which it absolutely did. Your salary notwithstanding, if you're happy with your career and you feel in control of your career destiny, you'll feel fulfilled in ways money can't provide.

Philosophy 5: Know what you're worth and honestly evaluate your strengths. If you feel like you're getting a raw deal from the big cheese and nothing else, let it be known and seek change.

In the years prior to being laid off, I wrote a book to be a bit creative and help strengthen my personal brand. I started doing more television segments and even dabbled in radio. I joined Facebook and started Tweeting. All this helped me remain relevant, boost my revenue stream, make me competitive in my professional realm, and enhance my network. Until my setback, however, I didn't recognize all of my behavior was actually part of a bigger personal philosophy on work and money. Once I was able to define it and lock it down, it was much easier to think about the future and feel empowered.

Guidelines for Crafting Your Financial Philosophies

When you feel fear or are in doubt about money or work, share those feelings with people you trust. The answers won't arrive at your front door unannounced.

A self-respecting person doesn't neglect credit card debt.

Save first, spend second.

A sale is not always a friend.

Some of the best things in life are free.

Money should be enjoyed (responsibly).

Opportunities to make money and advance your career are everywhere, but it's up to you to grab them.

Live beyond your means but spend within them.

Nobody cares about your money more than you.

The best investment is often a personal investment.

If you lend money, accept that you'll never see it returned.

Your generosity will pay off...with dividends.

Crafting Your Personal Money Philosophies

When crystallizing your own money beliefs, don't think that you have to limit each philosophy to one thought or one sentence. Clearly, I have many thoughts and points of view on the subject of money. Your philosophy or money mantra can be as short as a few bullets or pamphlet sized. It can be a combination of words and images. Your personal beliefs about money should reflect you, your values, and your sensibilities and strengths.

The three steps to crafting and maintaining your money philosophy are as follows:

Step 1: Recognize your values, which are often the same values you grew up with. These come from both nature and nurture. Our values are also ingrained in the commitments we deem most important to us in life, like family, marriage, career, staying healthy, and a commitment to our personal development and growth.

I asked one of my fiscally responsible friends and former colleague Allison, 33 and married, for her earliest childhood memory about money. What did she learn and why was it memorable?

I remember being so embarrassed as a child when my mom would drag us to the supermarket with her. We'd have a ridiculously full cart and head toward the checkout, where she'd whip out a stack of coupons (to be doubled, of course) and her checkbook. The line behind us would get longer and longer, and even as a kid I could read the body language of the people waiting impatiently behind us. It used to mortify me, and I remember barely being tall enough to reach the items on the counter, but I'd start bagging everything to speed the process along and end the embarrassment as fast as my little body would allow.

These memories are significant to me because when I entered college, no job, no car, no money, I realized that the best way to save money and still get the groceries that I needed was to use coupons and store membership programs. Now, as an adult, I've adopted it into my lifestyle, saving everywhere I can. I am an avid coupon clipper, surfing the fliers for sales and discounts, matching them up to the coupons that I have, knowing which stores will double the values (or sometimes triple!), and many times, getting all my household necessities for free or pennies. I don't allow us to carry any credit card debt.

Part of Allison's financial philosophy—which is to always look for deals, live below your means, and save whenever possible—is rooted in her upbringing. Her financial nurturing has also brought on other financial philosophies such as *don't allow thoughts of money to consume you* and *pay attention to the little things since they can add up.* She has chosen to see the benefits of being frugal, as opposed to holding on to the embarrassment as a child.

And that is the key takeaway with Allison's story. No matter how you were raised as a child around money, the adult thing to do is to look at it for what it was worth. What were the lessons it taught you, good and bad? What choices can you make now that you are in control of your own financial path to correct or build on the lessons ingrained in you as a kid? Allison continues by saying that "my parents and grandparents worked hard for their money. They scrimped and saved everywhere they could in order to splurge where it mattered. I adopted their philosophy on money and savings—and I'm really proud of it."

Allison describes her life as "financially stable" thanks to a deep-rooted and established belief system about money and how to manage it. She and her husband are committed to sticking to their mission statements. It's probably why Allison admits she is flirting with the idea of leaving her job. Someone without the security of savings and a commitment to her financial responsibilities wouldn't easily be able to do such a thing.

Conversely, memories and experiences from our childhood may not be how to properly craft financial philosophies. Sarah, a young 20-something retail associate, a subject on the *Bank of Mom & Dad*, remembers she and her mother always going on shopping sprees as a child. Very often, Sarah got what she wanted and would throw gigantic fits when she didn't. At one point, her mom remembers she had to drag her daughter out of the mall because she refused to buy her a dress.

Fast-forward 20-some years and Sarah is a self-described shopaholic (although she is recovering). One of her financial philosophies is that you have to "look the part in order to earn the part." She wants to be a professional designer and believes she needs to wear well-made and designer (i.e., expensive) clothing to make an impression on clients. I can see how appearances can make a positive difference in the workplace, but if you're like Sarah and you're racking up credit card debt to do so, you're not being responsible. You're not really fulfilling your philosophy. So the lesson here is that you may think you have established viewpoints, but do they work for you or against you? And if your perspective is causing you to fall into debt, how does that fit into your goals?

Step 2: Recognize your goals in life, everything to do with family, work, personal achievements, and relationships.

Step 3: Now tie in your working definition of *rich,* which you may still be pondering since reading the first chapter.

Now you're ready to develop as many personal *tenets* as you desire to help guide your decisions throughout your financial life. You'll find that some of your philosophies might not apply during the toughest of times, such as a divorce, a job loss, or a stock market crash, which is why it's helpful to have a few in your back pocket and refer to the ones that make the most sense given the circumstances.

At the same time, you must accept that your philosophies may transform over the course of your life. No matter how firm your views on money and no matter how well they're working for you, sometimes you need to make adjustments or commit to a backup philosophy. When you're younger, you may be more likely to embrace risk. As you age, however, you recognize the value in being more prudent and reserved with your cash. You should leave room for minor adjustments and growth because, after all, life (and our place in it) changes as time goes on.

For example, you may be someone who believes that you should splurge on what makes you happy. But if you lose your job and your income, you might need to put those splurges on hold for awhile, at least until you get back on your feet. During my unemployment hiatus, which ended up lasting a month or so, I used my time off to really buckle down and think about what I wanted to do, not what I *needed* to do. It was an opportunity to soul search (again!) at age 29 and reexamine my personal, professional, and financial ambitions. Thankfully, my finances weren't totally squeezed at that time—as I had sufficient savings—but an anxious voice in the back of my head kept asking, "What if you don't get steadily back on your feet in the next six months?" and more important, "What will you have to show for your time off?" Basically, my conscience was begging to know what my backup plan was, my Plan B. Well, my financial philosophy has one addendum that says "if all else fails, you can cash out the equity in your apartment and cast a wide net of jobs across a broad swath of fields and positions." What's important is that through a downturn, don't ever lose sight of your goals and try to "stay in the game" as much as possible.

4

Embrace Your Relationship with Money

"Money is not the most important thing in the world. Love is. Fortunately, I love money."

Jackie Mason, comedian

In any kind of relationship, you want to be confident and in control. You want to make sure you're being heard. You want clarity (and rightly so). Your relationship with money should be no different, yet this is something with which many of us struggle. And it's simple to see why. Money has been a taboo topic in our country for centuries.

Our upbringing influences how close we get with money and how honest our relationship with it becomes as adults. First impressions, as they turn out, hugely impact our subsequent decisions, including those related to money. If your parents never talked about money openly and never introduced you to the principles of saving, you may have a very disconnected relationship with money. From a macro perspective, too, money has yet to become a totally acceptable topic for wide-open discussion in our culture. We are more prone to talk about disease, sex, and marital conflict in the media than price tags, salaries, and credit card debt. The lack of financial literacy in schools and in homes is still another factor of this relationship weakness. And finally, because we encounter money issues somewhat infrequently (i.e., we don't deal with mortgages, car loans, and IRAs every day), it's hard to stay in touch and develop a level of comfort around finances.

The Money Heebie Jeebies

If you ask folks about their feelings toward money, their emotional response to even just the word *money* is a mix of anxiety, fear, desperation, and confusion. I have found this to be true even among those who make good salaries, have savings, and own a home.

In a recent poll, I asked people how money made them feel. The responses were largely negative, and many felt out of control. Jeff, a treasurer for an oil and gas company, says, "When I have a large amount of money, I feel warm and happy. When it's dwindling from spending, I get butterflies and feel disgusted and sick." Polly, a magazine editor, writes, "Money gives me excitement and lust for stuff when it comes my way… but overall fear that I'll mismanage it or that there won't be enough!" Michael, a teacher, says money makes him anxious. "Very anxious."

Partly to blame for this is our latest economic slide, no doubt. This dismal financial period in our country from late 2007 to the present has resulted in a near 10% unemployment rate, depleted investment accounts, millions of home foreclosures, and a lack of trust in institutions. How could we not be somewhat frightened? How can money make us feel safe when it could all be lost overnight?

But if we're being honest, our money emotions date further back than the latest economic slowdown. The recession may have just cemented existing fears and uncertainties about personal finance. Think back to your first job, your first paycheck, your first credit card statement, and the day you found out you didn't have enough financial aid to go to your dream college. What conversations about money did you have with your parents? With your friends? Most times, we deal and connect with money only when times are tough, when we need more of it, when we can't afford something. Therefore, when we go down memory lane, we remember the ugly stuff. But what about the good times?

After almost a decade of researching, writing, reporting, and coaching about money, I believe that we are still a long way from really finding the positive emotions related to money. We feel at a loss with our finances and indecisive at best, when actually the circumstances could be much, much better. Our money woes are not the result of an inability to understand budgeting pie charts or the evils of compound interest on a credit card. We know that our credit reports take a hit when we pay our bills late and that a little bit of savings here and there really adds up. The calculations and the mathematical reasoning behind sound financial management are available and widely known. So what gives? Why are we still a nation that can't get a grip on its finances?

There is something else holding us back, and for many of us it's not having the proper mindset or discipline to take money by the reins and establish the kind of financial life that we want. And then there's the emotional baggage.

Money Zombies

Gradually now, perhaps by force, we're getting better at our money relationships. With the recent flood of layoffs, investment losses, and foreclosures, Americans feel attacked by the financial world, and consumer confidence continues to lag. Through it all, we've been valiantly voicing our concerns and fighting to get a better handle on our finances. I call that both a silver lining and a work in progress. We're not totally at peace yet. Many of our emotional reactions to money and the thoughts surrounding our "money relationships" are negative, and that negativity is turning us into zombies. Here's why:

Lack of confidence. There's a severe lack of confidence when it comes to dealing with money, and that, in turn, becomes a huge psychological and emotional barrier as we try to get help, find solutions, and win our financial freedom. Money zombies are part of the "I'm not good at this stuff and I never will be" crowd. As a result, many of us do nothing; we become paralyzed and end up living paycheck to paycheck because we just don't have the confidence to take control of our finances and aim higher. The fact is, there's a lot of shame around money, and so long as we continue to believe we're not good enough or we're not capable enough to help ourselves, the further we drown in our shame and the more susceptible we become to damaging our finances.

Apathy. Those who are apathetic often think "why bother?" These are the people inflicted with a sense of defeat before any financial move takes place, folks who in their minds just can't win when it comes to championing their finances. They see no point in doing so either since they can't fight "the system." *Why bother* investing money in the stock market if it's all going to dissolve in the next recession? *Why bother* paying off my credit card if they're just going to settle pennies on the dollar? *What's in it for me?*

My Story:
Bad Credit...So What!

At Loyola University in Chicago, during one of my college visits this year, a brazen senior sitting in the back row of the auditorium raised his hand to ask, "Why bother paying off my credit cards? What's the worst that'll happen? Is it just that it will get reported on my credit report?" Just? Wasn't that consequence enough? I couldn't tell whether this guy just wanted to put me on the spot or if he was seriously questioning why he should follow the rules.

I played along. "Your credit report will be stained for about seven years if you default on your credit cards, which will make it tougher for you to borrow money for a car, a house, or a business in the future," I explained to him and to the crowd. That's bad enough, right?

The young man in the back was not impressed. He wanted to hear about potential torture and pain, the possibility of losing your house, losing your car, serious and painful consequences. Would he prefer American Express take his firstborn child in the event of being 60 days past due? (Sometimes I wish those were the terms. I happen to think fear plays an effective role for some in getting their financial act together. More on that later.)

On the one hand, this apparent-masochist had a point. Credit card companies don't necessarily come after you for the wrinkle-free khakis you charged on your Gap card and never paid off. They don't drive to your house and take away your college diploma (since 30% of students are now carrying tuition balances on credit cards). But if push comes to shove, you could very well get sued in some cases for neglecting to pay your debt. You might have legal costs on top of your other financial troubles to deal with. And who wants that? A show of hands? Masochist Mickey quieted down and left early. He didn't even grab a free book or some cookies. I'm hoping it was because he was so anxious to get back to his dorm to make an overdue Visa payment online.

Addiction. Then there are money addicts. These aren't people who are addicted to *making* money. It's actually just the opposite: people who are addicted to spending money to reach an emotional or psychological high they need and fill a void in their life. Addicts don't usually think they're addicts (the first sign of being an addict). With money addicts, the first tell-tale sign is thinking they're not the only one who has a spending or a savings problem. They rationalize what they're doing by saying, "Well, I'm not the only one having a hard time." That's according to Terri Ciochetti, a licensed psychotherapist and financial counselor in Southern California for the past decade. She specializes in studying people's relationships with their money. During the recession, she noticed more of her clients coming to her confessing their financial difficulties, but with the attitude that "well, the world is having a hard time," so it's not just me. They frighteningly believed their overspending and undersaving was just a phase, despite years and years of the same struggles. "That's a common addict's approach," says

Terri, "the it's not me, it's them mentality." For addicts, taking ownership of their problems and coming to terms with their reality is the first step toward recovery.

Money Harmony

Constructing a Healthier Connection

A colleague of mine, Atefeh, a CFA with a degree in psychology, tells me in all honesty that "money makes me anxious because I always fear it will run out…I have the need to both make money and save it, so I never end up enjoying it…I know there has to be a happy medium."

Well, there is a happy medium. Just as in any relationship, there are compromises. Married folks, like my parents, will tell you this. But as long as there is a commitment to the relationship, a willingness to work hard, be patient, and make careful decisions, your relationship can be a healthy one. As we know in so many other realms of life, the mind that says "I can do it" can help us achieve anything, including financial bliss.

Identifying What's Not Working

Since so many of us are in the dumps about money, it's important to first isolate what about the relationship is troubling you. If you don't feel in control, what needs to change? If you're anxious, what do you need to do feel more certain about? If you don't feel confident, why are you insecure?

To know the details of your money picture is to know yourself. First, you need to understand what your lifestyle is today and what you want it to be in the future. What is, in fact, your mission statement for life? What are your values, your hopes, your dreams? What ethics do you follow? What inspires you? What do you know about yourself (your strengths and weaknesses)? This process of identifying what's not working is similar to your thought process before entering a serious relationship with another person. It helps to know what you want out of it, what you're going to give back, and how you plan to keep the relationship thriving.

Reconnecting

You can reestablish your relationship with money in the following four ways:

1. **Focus on the good.** Feeling appreciative of your financial situation, despite some of the possible setbacks you're facing, is one way to improve your relationship with money. Terri says this is a behavioral exercise that often helps her clients. "I'm hearing people having a little bit more appreciation for the fact that they have a job, they have a home and live indoors. As people have more appreciation, feelings of depravation can diminish." If you're trying to feel more appreciative of your money and develop a closer relationship in that sense, it's important to surround yourself with people who share your beliefs and values.

2. **Reflect on earlier years.** To transition out of any of bad relationships with money, Terri agrees with me that the first step is to explore our earliest connections with money. How did our upbringing leave an impression? What did our parents teach us (or neglect to teach us) about money? What do you want to change about the past? Just as we did this to formulate our philosophy on money, it's important to do so when trying to find peace with your relationship with money.

3. **Roll up your sleeves.** To connect with your money, you need to do it on a regular basis and in as many ways as possible. "Until people get very hands on with their money—tracking it, keeping account of how it's spent, analyzing where their money's gone, their values and expectations—they're stuck," Terri says.

4. **Let fear make you stronger.** Fear is a major emotion when it comes to our finances. Some of us fear failure (losing our jobs),

some fear dependency (being in a marriage and not having any financial knowledge or wherewithal), and some fear the unknown (a sudden market crash). And I dare say that having a little fear in your money relationship can go a long, long way. At the least, it may prevent you from making the choices that will lead you to your worst nightmare.

In general, we never want to imagine bad things happening. We want to think that some supernatural force will protect us from evil. But in life, the unexpected happens. And although "preparing for the unexpected" may sound oxymoronic, you can, in fact, ensure that you have various options available when the "unforeseen" becomes the "seen." And wouldn't you like to be prepared to deal with or possibly even avoid the negative ramifications of life's difficulties?

The same is true when it comes to money. We'd like to think that our jobs will always be there, that our savings will be protected forever, that our homes will only appreciate in value. But people do lose their jobs and their savings, they get robbed, scammed, divorced, they fall sick without health insurance, all things with major financial repercussions. A little fear can help you face these possible realities and prepare for the worst. It can inspire you to take control and change bad financial habits.

I expect some of you disagree with my notion about fear and money. We know that fear can get in the way of us getting ahead in life. But fear of financial disaster can yield positive results when it is coupled with awareness: a wakefulness to the potential tough times that are the consequences of certain actions and choices. You want to get to a place where you can say, "I would never want that to happen to me!" After that, you will be prompted to take more responsible action. For what it's worth, Terri agrees with my theory on fear. Channeling your fear is sometimes very helpful, she tells me, because "you're imagining hitting rock bottom and what it feels like to be stuck and really in trouble."

My Story: Facing Up to Reality

In one of my episodes of Bank of Mom & Dad, *I worked with a sweet young woman named Julie. Julie was a former NFL cheerleader who had a serious amount of debt—close to $30,000—stemming from an over-the-top car loan, unpaid bills, and of course, credit card debt from clothes, eating out, and jewelry she couldn't necessarily afford.*

While a cheerleader, Julie was accustomed to the "good life," but she also had a boyfriend who paid for most of her expenses. Despite the fact that her cheering days and open-wallet boyfriend were over, 28-year-old Julie insisted on holding on to the past. Even though she was earning a smaller salary at her part-time dental assistant job, she continued to charge ahead (literally) with her previous lifestyle and tastes.

Less than a year into her post-cheerleading life, she was begging her mom and her older brother for some financial SOS, and for a while, they obliged. Mom took money out of her pension to assist Julie with her bills. Chad, her older brother, let Julie live in his apartment rent free.

Julie's goals included becoming financially independent, but she didn't have a plan. I suspect it was because she was banking on marrying a wealthy man and becoming a housewife, like some of her cheerleader girlfriends had. Julie admitted this during the show, and even her mom and brother acknowledged that Julie had dependency issues on men that kept her from seeking her own financial independence. But Prince Charming isn't coming, we all explained to Julie. And if he does, that will just be icing on top. In the meantime, you still need to get your financial act together and assume responsibility in your life.

What Julie didn't quite realize at the time is the help you get from friends and family has limits. It's only temporary. At some point, family and friends will get fed up with our mooching ways. And that's exactly what happened to Julie. Her mother and brother came on the show to say they would not be able to continue helping her out. I asked Julie to consider some scary consequences: What are you going to do when the money stops coming in from your mom? What's going to happen when Chad says you can't sleep on his couch anymore? What if your knight in shining armor with his fat bank account never comes to rescue you? It's going to get really ugly, I explained.

So let's imagine the consequences. How would she like to sleep in her car? What would it feel like to declare bankruptcy? The thoughts hadn't ever entered Julie's head, and so this sudden encounter with fear first made her cry (and made me feel really bad). But then it led her to face her responsibilities once and for all.

Did she change overnight? Of course not. But the progress reports I've been getting from both Julie and her mom suggest she's truly beginning to pick up the financial pieces in her life and actually enjoying the process. She has found the motivation to make better choices that will steer her away from complete financial ruin. She has found a second part-time job, moved into her own apartment (with an ugly, used couch, but nonetheless "it's my *couch," she writes), and has completely paid off one of her credit cards. She's not out of the woods entirely yet, but she now realizes that she is the only one who is going to get herself out of the ugly mess she created (and has the will to do so).*

Moral Obligations in Your Relationship?

Some of you might immediately roll your eyes at this topic: morality and money. Do the two even belong in the same sentence? Do you have any moral or ethical obligations to the financial choices you make? This is not something we think about often. However, your views about such influence your decision making, especially during tough times. So, you want to know what your views are, right?

One way to analyze this is to consider a hot topic: your home mortgage (and think of that as a subrelationship to the overall relationship you have with your money at large). Lots of Americans locked themselves into risky mortgages over the past decade, and as home values depreciated over the past few years, many began to question the benefits to staying in a financial relationship in which they felt they were getting a raw deal. Should you just walk away or continue to make payments on a depreciated asset? You understand that your credit will take a hit for seven years or so, and securing any further loans will be pretty much impossible in the near future. But if your mortgage is eating away at your ability to live a stable life and fulfill your other financial obligations, is this a relationship you should kick to the curb?

Last year, I received that very question from a distressed reader, Michael, who was wondering whether he should stay or just give up and walk away from his three-bedroom home in Detroit, Michigan. His main gripe—like some eight million Americans at the time—was that his home was valued much lower than the amount of his mortgage. So, should he just stop paying and let the bank deal with it since he isn't building any equity and probably won't at any point in the foreseeable future? Apparently, most Americans would stay put, according to a recent survey of 1,000 U.S. homeowners; only 15% of Americans believe financial distress is a good enough reason to walk away from their underwater mortgages.[1] Those who would stay put would consider other options, like trying to modify their loan, selling the property, and renting out a room to help make ends meet. In that same survey, a third of respondents said moral obligations would convince them to continue paying an underwater mortgage.

In Michael's situation, he had an extremely high interest rate of 8.6%, making his monthly principal plus interest payment roughly $1,850 (more than half his monthly income). In addition, Detroit was suffering from the highest unemployment and foreclosure rates in the country at the time, so the chances of a quick market recovery there were not likely. "The area is starting to decline due to many vacant or vandalized homes, with several break-ins, three for myself," he wrote to me. Michael's credit was already poor (hence the 8.6% rate), but on the flip side he no longer used his credit cards. He and his wife were on a cash diet.

More middle-of-the-road homeowners are grappling with the same issue as Michael, not necessarily because they can't *afford* their monthly payments, but because they are "underwater," owing more on their mortgage than the home is currently worth. They're not building any equity, and when time comes to sell, they'll probably be in the hole. The IRS has also made it less of a tax pain to give up on your mortgage by now offering special tax relief for financially strapped borrowers who lose their home due to foreclosure. Prior to this, so-called forgiven debt was considered taxable income.

The Fixed-Income Team at Credit Suisse noted at the end of 2009 that "should the downward spiral in home prices, neighborhood condition, and equity deterioration continue, more and more main-stream borrowers are likely to walk away from their homes." Credit Suisse also predicted that more than eight million mortgages would enter into foreclosure over the next four years. That's about 16% of all mortgages.

In Michael's case, it's obvious he should definitely move to a safer neighborhood. Three break-ins in one month is more than enough reason to leave. But should he *abandon* his mortgage? I asked some experts to weigh in with some analysis: Wall Street economist Joe Brusuelas; Gerri Detweiler, a credit advisor for Credit.com; and Jon Maddux, CEO and co-founder of YouWalkAway.com, a site that helps distressed homeowners learn about their alternatives, such as ditching their mortgage. For a $1,000 fee, YouWalkAway guides you through the process. Before getting started, the website offers an online calculator that helps you mathematically decide whether it's a good idea to walk away from your mortgage. To them, some financial commitments justifiably call for a split.

Joe said that in general he was not a fan of walking away from a mortgage, but in certain cases he said abandoning your mortgage sometimes make sense. It's an exception, not a rule, and sometimes you'll find, after close examination, that it's not even a matter of ethics. "There may be a narrow range of conditions under which walking away from a home that is so far underwater, it's absolutely rational," Joe tells me.

Breaking Up

Here are some of the factors our experts say are extremely important to consider before deciding to walk away from this specific money relationship. And in any sticky situation like this, you may want to get legal help from a bankruptcy attorney.

Your bank won't help. The bottom line is, banks don't want to go through another foreclosure process. It takes time and money. But if playing scared and saying you desperately need to modify your loan or *else* fails to earn you any material help, consider it a sign you have to take matters into your own hands, which may require walking away. And before you do, make sure your bank also has no plans to chase you down and sue you for "deficiency" claims, says Gerri Detweiler of Credit.com, which, depending on your situation, could end up costing thousands and thousands of dollars. Some states, such as California and Florida, now prohibit deficiency claims, and in other states some lenders are choosing not to go after defaulted borrowers because they've got too much else on their plates. But, "until the statute of limitations is expired, I wouldn't think I was in the clear," says Detweiler. "The lenders may come after you in a couple of years after taking a deep breath." Some attorneys recommend getting a signed letter from your bank stating it won't sue you for deficiency claims.

You're not able to save or address your other immediate money relationships. Of the 5,000+ members (at the time of this writing) who've so far signed on to YouWalkAway.com, many have decided to forgo their mortgage because they say they're no longer able to save any money. "They see [their home] as a major drain to their savings and cash flow in general. They don't want to keep bleeding, basically," says CEO Jon Maddox. If every payment on your mortgage is a step backward from achieving your other top financial goals, like saving, putting food on the table for your family, and paying down your other debt, a foreclosure, he says, may be a suitable path, especially if you don't see the area appreciating in value in the next five, seven, or ten years.

You're okay with damaging your credit. A foreclosure stains your credit report for seven years, much like Chapter 13 bankruptcy, which is a partial debt repayment plan. A Chapter 7 bankruptcy, which eliminates your debt entirely, sits on your credit report for ten years. Despite foreclosures becoming more common, don't expect any lender to cut you a break. "Ultimately, lenders make decision based on risk," says Detweiler. "Lenders really shy away from serious negative items like foreclosure and bankruptcy." It will take at least a few years before you can qualify for a new loan, and your rates will be extremely high. To put it in economic terms, "Your credit score is going to limit your opportunities for consumption and your choice matrix," says Brusuelas. Another tip: Don't let the potential consequences on your credit report decide between filing for a foreclosure or a bankruptcy. They're both quite ugly. Instead, examine the bigger picture. Determine what your future goals are and what the best personal strategy may be for you. And talk to a bankruptcy attorney to weigh all your options. "The homeowner needs to focus on what is the best financial strategy for the next, say, five years, versus trying to beat the credit scoring system," says Detweiler.

You're otherwise "okay" with it. This is where your conscience can potentially take the steering wheel. The decision to walk away from your home has been chastised in some press for being "immoral." A contract is a promise, some critics argue, and therefore should be upheld no matter what. It's an obligation, plain and simple. What's more, foreclosing on your home potentially lowers the value of the neighborhood and hurts the value of your neighbor's home and the stability of the overall economy. Are you okay with that? University of Arizona law school professor Brent T. White wrote in a controversial paper titled "Underwater and Not Walking Away: Shame, Fear and the Social Management of the Housing Crisis," that if it was in their best financial interests, homeowners should consider ditching their mortgage and not worry about the "moral hazard."

Maddox agrees, telling me there's no moral obligation to keeping an unfavorable mortgage, considering if all the above holds true. Desperate mortgage holders should do what they can to help themselves get out of a painful situation, especially when their bank won't compromise or modify the loan. That means considering all alternatives: renting out a room, selling the house for a loss, and yes, even walking way. After all, he says, banks have no problem breaking contracts or writing off assets. "If banks cut their bottom line by, for example, firing workers, they get applauded by shareholders. But guys struggling to pay for their kids' college because their mortgage is too high, those guys get thrown under the bus and we say they're deadbeats, unethical, and immoral."

Breaking up is never easy. Before parting ways—whether it's with a mortgage, a financial advisor, or a particular bank—you need to evaluate the pros and cons, as well as the consequences on your finances and on your stability.

Family, Friends, and Money

Friends and family can be a serious money drain, and it helps to be able to stand up for yourself when the pressure's on to lend. Experts Jeanne Fleming and Leonard Schwarz, *Money* magazine columnists and authors of *Isn't It Their Turn to Pick Up the Check?*, have done a great deal of research on the subject. They found 60% of the public admitted that in every family, there's always someone who's constantly asking for money, the "serial borrowers." As times get tougher, they will see this "as a golden opportunity to do what they always do, namely put their hands out and whine," say the authors.

Here's how to stay in control of the situation:

Be open-minded. Being an advocate for your money in scenarios where you are asked to lend money doesn't mean always saying no. It means, first and foremost, assessing the situation and the potential borrower. If this certain someone has lent you money in the past, you're sort of obligated to try to return the favor. Consider a few things, including the closeness of your relationship, how likely it is you'll get the money back, and why this person needs money in the first place. Is it to help pay a mortgage? Or to buy a new cell phone (when he already has two)? Knowing how your money will be spent should be a big determining factor for you, the potential lender.

Be okay with never seeing the money returned. It's never a good idea to lend money that you can't afford to live without. Fleming and Schwarz's research shows that 43% of the largest loans people make in their lives are not repaid in full, and with 27% of them, the lender gets nada. Before lending anyone money, think about whether you can realistically and emotionally afford to make the loan a gift.

For big loans, get a contract. For amounts that exceed, say, $500, or an amount that you absolutely, unequivocally need to get back in the near future, have a contract that lists the borrower's and lender's information, including names, addresses, social security numbers, and so forth. Then describe the loan agreement: the dollar amount of the loan, the repayment schedule, and any interest you may want to charge. Virgin-Money.com is the largest social loan facilitator in the country and helps contract and manage private loans between peers. They've processed more than $450 million in social loans since launching in 2007. If you have a loan with a family member, friend, or a business partner, and it's at least a few hundred dollars, Virgin Money's services (starting at around $99) might make sense. You can also enlist the help of an attorney you pay by the hour to draft the contract and set up the repayment process. Working with a third-party—either online or offline—not only keeps you organized, but it helps to take some emotion out of the deal.

If the answer is no, present alternatives. It's hard to say no, but remember that the conversation doesn't need to abruptly end at N-O. There are alternatives to cash. Direct them to peer-to-peer lending sites like LendingClub.com, where you can apply for an individual loan in the public marketplace. Or perhaps you know a financial advisor who can help them acquire a loan from a local bank, or maybe go with them to apply for a loan. If your friend or family member gets rejected, don't stop there. Make a plan to visit at least three banks and credit unions. Another alternative to giving money is to offer your help in the form of time and services. If your cousin or best friend needs $500 to make ends meet this month, offer to cook dinners, drive her to work, or watch her kids for free. If she needs a new suit for an interview, let her shop in your closet. There are numerous ways to help without actually writing a check.

When Love Strikes

Whether you are dating, in a partnership, or married, money can play an enormous role in the union. Couples say spending is the cause of the most serious conflicts in marriage, specifically lack of communication (including not discussing goals or knowing each other's money habits, both good and bad). Married couples have about a 45% chance of divorcing over money-related issues, according to the *New York Times*.[2] More likely than not, your partner will have a different relationship with money than you do…and that's okay. Terri, who meets with couples on a regular basis, explains that the important thing is that you both recognize your similarities and your differences as early on as possible, agree to common goals, and accept that you will both do what you have to do support those goals. "If we don't talk about it and instead just make assumptions, that makes for a very difficult road." And just like sex, she adds, if you can't talk about it, you shouldn't do it.

In a MyFico.com survey, one-third of respondents said that a lack of financial responsibility hurt their relationships more than being unfaithful (22%), a lack of affection (21%), or a lack of a sense of humor (16%).[3] Problems paying bills late was cited as often as problems with in-laws or relatives as the most stressful situations that put pressure on a relationship. Credit.com's Gerri Detweiler, my go-to credit expert, says the stats speak volumes about how important it is to be on the same financial page as your partner. And the sooner the better. She says 20% of divorces occur within the first five years of a marriage. "Clearly, a good income and financial stability can help a marriage, and the opposite can hurt it. While some couples draw closer together during times of crisis, many won't survive financial woes," says Gerri. "Going into a marriage with different views about money can spell disaster." She cites a few studies with glaring evidence. One from the University of California found that money was the major source of disagreement for close to 250 newlywed couples in their first and third years of marriage.[4] And based on a survey by researchers at Utah State University, tying the knot before clearing yourself of debt has a harmful impact on "newlywed levels of marital quality."[5]

You should try everything you can to get financially in sync, and I'll be the first to say that's easier said than done. How to come out and just discuss money? For starters, you don't have to be so direct about it (at first). Terri offers us some easy exercises to, as she explains, "meet *around* money." For example, consider reading a money book together (maybe this one!) or going to a seminar and sharing your notes afterward.

If after much discussion and perhaps even therapy you find that your goals are not aligned and never will be and that is weighing on your happiness and your ability to live your life, you have to seriously think about whether you can afford this relationship.

Before you commit, before walking down the aisle and signing that marriage license, you should know each other's money strengths and weaknesses, as well as your short- and long-term goals. Admittedly, while dating, it might not feel all that appropriate to ask personal questions about money.

Here are my favorite icebreakers to help open discussions as the respondent begins to go down memory lane:

How did you pay your way through college? Or, how did you afford college?

You may discover you both have tens of thousands of dollars in student loans or a great big credit card bill that's carrying debt from college. Maybe he or she skipped college and has no debt at all. Dig deeper and discover how both of you are dealing with your loans and how you are managing to find work without a degree. After about six months of dating, my boyfriend and I disclosed our "debt" loads, and it started with a conversation about college loans, which was the easiest to talk about since nearly everyone with a college degree has dealt with this at some point. I discovered he had paid off his loans already like I had. He didn't have all that much when he graduated and aggressively paid off the remaining amount within the first few years after graduating. I had used a lump sum of cash from my first book advance to pay down all my remaining student loans both from Penn State and Columbia, where I went to grad school.

What is your earliest memory of money?

This is a great question because it could provide some insight into this person's perception or value of money and his or her nurtured influence. My friend Dave, a 34-year-old dad of two, remembers growing up in a very financially conservative household. At age 7, his parents explained to the kids what "basic necessities" were: food, shelter, and clothing. Anything above and beyond that would have to come out of an allowance, which as Dave recalls, "didn't amount to much week over week." This led him to become extremely patient with money and learn how to delay gratification. He remembers obsessing over a Transformers action figure and having to wait months before he could afford it. "The reason this is so memorable," he says, "is because that's a tough lesson to learn from the point of view of a child...To save took a lot of dedication and drive." As an adult, Dave's saving skills protected his family when he became unemployed in 2009 for almost an entire year. "I always pay myself first by putting the most I can manage into a savings account and losing the account number at least until the next paycheck!"

Do you rent or do you own?

A conversation about real estate is often one of the best ways to get into some serious money conversations. If the answer is "I rent," ask whether he or she has ambitions to ever own a home and why or why not. It's a loaded question that may bring up signs of financial stability or insecurities about the market and their own finances. If this person has tackled the real estate market and owns a property, that's a pretty impressive sign, assuming he or she is current with the mortgage (by the way, a good thing to find out).

Where do you want to be in a few years?

It's a perfectly natural question to want to know the direction your partner is headed or *wants* to lead. For example, do you want to save up for a house, a big trip, your own business? All of these milestones have price tags, and it's important to know whether you would support these goals once in a committed relationship with this person.

What's your number?

And I don't mean phone digits. I mean, what would be a comfortable salary for you to live on? This might not be first-date conversation, but as you two grow closer, this may be a strategic way to open a dialogue about what it means to be "financially comfortable." Use this question as a gateway to then talk further about money values, long-term goals, and what it means to feel rich.

What's your credit like?

This is probably the most important question…but it's not kosher to ask this straight out on date one or even date number two. This is a topic you want to gauge when you feel the relationship is getting serious or if you see the two of you investing in or purchasing anything together. And if you want my advice: Hold off on cosigning anything for each other until you're married and/or prepared to accept the risk that your partner may not follow through on your joint financial obligations.

My friend Karina is married and house hunting, but has decided not to apply for a mortgage jointly with her husband Sam. The reason? Sam has poor credit, and the couple is worried his less-than-stellar track record might weigh down their chances of getting a good interest rate. The downside is that they will not qualify for as big of a loan because the bank will base it on Karina's salary alone. They figure they'll live in a smaller house until Sam improves his credit score and then try again down the road for a new, bigger home.

And after all those questions and answers, still keep your eyes open!

Finally, be observant about how your partner spends and manages money. Is he or she using cash or plastic all the time? Does your partner track his or her spending at all? Good tipper or bad tipper? Generous with his or her money? Does your partner talk about money so much it makes you want to scream? Or the opposite, which also makes you wonder?

It's easy to overlook money issues when you are in love because talking about money is not romantic. Also, it's not something that we as a culture talk very openly about. We're more likely to disclose intimate details about previous relationships, our health, and our jobs than our credit score or the number of loans under our name. So, the best advice here is when you want to combine your money relationships, be straightforward about it as much as you can, but in a nonthreatening way and when you're both in a good mood. If you start feeling strain on the financial relationship you share, go first to each other for guidance. See what adjustments each may need to make to spending and saving. Designate one person (the one who's most organized) to be the chief financial officer in the household. All the while, keep the other partner involved. And trade responsibilities once in a while so that no one's kept in the dark.

And a final thought from Terri: "Best to do all of this before kids enter the picture."

[1] Fannie Mae National Housing Survey, April 2010.

[2] Ron Leiber, "Money Talks to Have Before Marriage," *New York Times*, October 23, 2009.

[3] MyFico.com and The Heart/Credit Connection, "Personal Shortcomings" survey, 2006.

[4] Jean Roggins, "Topics of Marital Disagreement Among African-American and Euro-American Newlyweds," University of California at San Francisco, 2003.

[5] Lisa Skogrand, David Schramm, James Marshall, and Thomas Lee, "The Effects of Debt on Newlyweds and Implications for Education," Utah State University, 2005.

Part II

Psych It Up

5 ──────────────────────

Organize. Don't Agonize

"Once you have a clear picture of your priorities—that is values, goals, and high-leverage activities—organize around them."

Stephen Covey, author of *The 7 Habits of Highly Effective People*

Why do I invest so much time and money at the Container Store? Why do I feel like I "need" a Lazy Susan turntable and another shoe rack? As a society, many of us strive to get our lives neatly organized, as evidenced by our spice racks, DVD shelves, and tax folders. Spring cleaning in the winter? I'm so there. But does all this organization really create Zen?

Well, have you ever been to the Container Store? For me, I can honestly say it's a form of heaven on earth. I can (and have) spent hours cruising through the chain store's glorious aisles of Elfa installation components and desktop organizers, imagining how they'll bring peace and serenity to my life. And when my bed is made and my kitchen is clean, I certainly do feel more at ease. And I'm not alone. My friend and organization professional Jodi Watson, the founder of Supreme Organization, tells me that organization helps us stay balanced, clear, and focused. Not to mention, it makes us more self-confident and efficient in our day-to-day lives. (Just as long as your Container Store addiction doesn't deplete your bank account.)

Getting Squared Away

Messiness is distracting. Benjamin Franklin wisely said that "for every minute spent organizing, an hour is earned." Conversely, a lack of organization can stir up anxiety, confusion, and a feeling of helplessness. When it comes to your finances, a lack of a system or strategy is nearly ten times worse because you're not only sacrificing your peace of mind but you're potentially sacrificing your financial well-being.

The four words I hear most commonly from people inundated with bills and credit card statements are these: *Where do I begin?* That is, how do I start taking care of this mess and turn it into something that makes clear sense and is easy to reference?

My Story: Junk Drawer Diaries

Danielle, a great case study on Bank of Mom & Dad, *was raised by a very organized mom who had a system for all her financial paperwork and bills, yet Danielle struggled to manage her own finances. She couldn't tell you how much her cable bill was last month because she lost the statement or never even opened the bill. She had a disastrous kitchen drawer of unopened envelopes from creditors, in addition to crinkled-up receipts. It had become so overwhelming that Danielle just opted to ignore it. She became a financial zombie. As a result, bills got paid late or never at all. Along the way, she struggled to make ends meet for herself and for her family. Her money would run out before the end of the month (and without her having a clue as to where it all went). Interestingly enough, Danielle was an extremely talented woman when it came to managing and organizing other aspects of her life, from caring for her baby daughter to growing her small fashion business. When it came to money, however, she just didn't know, to put it in her words, where to begin. She felt defeated before ever making any real effort to solve the problem.*

Luckily for Danielle and everyone else who feels lost, three clear-cut steps can help you put your financial life in order (and they're primarily mental). First and foremost, take a mental inventory of your life and understand your obligations and goals. Second, cut the clutter from your life; *clutter* here refers to the emotional distractions that keep you from addressing your obligations and goals. The difficulty, of course, is that humans have a tough time letting go of most things. Dan Ariely, behavioral economist and author of *Predictably Irrational,* says the reason for this is that we simply prefer to keep our options open. "It's very hard to close doors," Ariely tells me. Choosing what should stay and what should go from our lives is not easy. "Closing a door is saying here's an option that I'll never have for life. It's a very hard choice," he says. The final piece in achieving an organized financial life is to establish the right habits and stay committed. Let's examine how these steps play out in reality.

Step 1. Take Inventory: Priorities and Goals

Whenever you feel like you've lost a grip on your finances, stop and remind yourself of your obligations and goals. Maybe you've fallen off course, racked up a bit of debt, and now find yourself asking how you get here. And more important, you might be asking, how do I get out of this mess? To address this problem, you must first remember who you are and what you want in life.

If you were to organize your inventory of obligations and goals, what would the list look like? I asked my friend Dave for his list. You met him in the previous chapter. He's the married father of two whose early days of saving up for a Transformer taught him how to delay gratification.

Dave's Personal Priorities:

1. Provide for and protect my family: wife and kids (have money for food, clothes, health expenses, saving, and so on).

2. Protect our home (pay the mortgage and real estate taxes).

3. Save for our retirement (invest in our 401k, IRA, and other retirement savings vehicles).

4. Enjoy life (have enough money for fun like eating out, travel, entertainment, and so forth).

Dave's Professional Priorities:

1. Understand and fulfill the requirements at work.

2. Grow my career as well as the business of the company.

3. Watch for opportunities and focus on professional areas that may be beyond my current understanding.

Dave's Personal Goals:

1. Travel more, specifically to Ireland, Greece, Italy, and St. Barts.

2. Expand my family and have a couple more kids.

Dave's Professional Goals:

1. Move up the corporate ladder to become an officer of a company.

2. Continue to grow a side career in real estate.

3. Start my own business in real estate.

Knowing where you currently stand with obligations and goals and where you eventually want to stand will allow you to build an organizational structure to help realize those aspirations. It all goes back to the notion that if you understand your goals and consciously and actively strive for them to become reality, you'll more easily guide your money toward the appropriate channels. For example, with his inventory of priorities and goals established, Dave is unlikely to invest all his savings toward starting his own business in real estate, even though it's a top goal, before he has addressed his mortgage and his retirement savings. As Dave says, "In order to accomplish my goals, I find myself managing my money a lot more conservatively than I have in the past and trying to understand my needs versus my wants."

Step 2. Clear the Clutter

The next step is to clear the clutter out of your life. And I'm not talking about clutter such as two-year-old receipts from the now-defunct Circuit City and your tax forms from 1992. To cut the clutter out of your financial life, you need to eliminate the conscious and unconscious distractions that do absolutely nothing to support your financial obligations and your goals. From mooching friends to unstable relationships to peer pressure and social expectations to look and act a certain way, clutter is all around us, and it is not helping you in the financial department.

> *What's the unnecessary drama that's preventing you from putting your life in perspective, from getting a hold on your finances and making sense out of it all? You want to identify it and get it out of your system.*

Part of Danielle's clutter was a lack of self-esteem. She had just gotten laid off from her dream job working for a fashion design house in New York City and had no new job prospects. The layoff had forced her move back to her hometown of Hartford, Connecticut, where life was more affordable. There she was struggling to re-create her New York City life with her husband and 2-year-old daughter. Depression was eating away at her ability to properly manage her financial house. How did she ultimately snap out of it? Well, she wasn't exactly in denial of her disorganized ways. She also knew she was having a hard time dealing with unemployment. So, she was very much aware of her financial problems. For Danielle, visualization and seeking a mentor were the two vital forces that helped her change her ways.

First, she began to set up visual reinforcements of her goals around her home. Because she is a creative person, this was a fun exercise for her, and she took it really far. She created a board of visual elements to remind herself why it's important to stay financially on track. She included pictures of her baby daughter, her family, fabric swatches, and a list of bills she needed to address right away. She left the board hanging in her kitchen, knowing people would ask her about it and that she'd be prompted to share...and down the road she would feel accountable to those people and would want to make them proud. Another helpful technique was to seek the mentorship of Byron Lars, a designer she had always looked up to. Danielle had always admired his success but never quite knew the sweat and tears behind the scenes. Getting in touch with him and sharing her goals, as well as her financial struggles, earned her a much-needed advocate and a trusted source to help her follow through on her goals.

Understanding the Signs

Jack, a 29-year-old aspiring fitness guru, spent almost $11,000 last year on his image: athletic clothing, sneakers, and tanning. That's in addition to money he spent on marketing, rental space at athletic facilities, and training equipment. He argued the clothes and the tan were a necessary investment to project a certain image that would score clients. Okay, I understand that. But did he have to buy $150 sneakers every three months? And really, $500 a month for tanning? Although he might have had a great tan to show for it all at the end of the month, his business wasn't growing that much. What was growing, however, was his debt. Jack looked amazing on the outside but was a financial mess on the inside. What was really driving his compulsive shopping, as it turns out, was not so much the desire to boost his business, but the need to feed his self-confidence and self-image. I understand that self-confidence and image are components of a successful business, but I don't accept that they have to come at an annual expense of $11,000 for material things that ultimately keep you in a cycle of debt.

The fact was, Jack's obsession with appearance was clutter. It was fogging up his ability to focus on what really mattered, which was building relationships with clients, getting his certifications, and of course, getting out of debt so that he could manage a profitable business sooner rather than later. To cut this clutter, he needed to think long term and accept that at this rate of spending he would not be able to get his business off the ground.

The Working-Mother Dilemma

Another example of how clutter or inner drama can damage one's ability to organize financial obligations and goals is the mother who works full-time and rarely says no to her kids' wishes. She's put their needs and wants before hers, which ends up causing a lot of financial drama in this mom's life.

One of my clients, let's call her Rita, feels she neglects her kids during the week, working 60 hours at her PR office and arriving home in time just to give baths and read bedtime stories. Her guilt translates into not being able to say no to her children, even while knowing she should teach them to delay gratification. On weekends, it's constant pampering, toy store visits, and dessert before dinner. Money just pours out of her wallet to make up for lost time and attention during the week. It's safe to say Rita is not organized in terms of having a firm grip on her goal and priorities. Certainly a goal is not to raise spoiled children. And although one of her goals has been to begin saving money to afford a vacation sometime soon, all her disposable income has been going toward the kids' expenses. Rita's not alone. Women generally fail to put themselves (and their financial needs) first.

Marcia Brixey, author of *The Money Therapist,* told me, "Women are nurturers and caregivers. We take care of everyone else but ourselves and it hinders us later in life." So how can Rita and other mothers get their financial lives in order and kill this guilt?

First, they must alter their perspective and focus on the positive aspects of having their kids see them as the ultimate multitasker, which Rita certainly is. If this is you, you need to change the way you view your decision to be a mom who works full time. Be proud of the fact that you are able to provide for your family. Second, communicate your message by explaining your choice to work to your family and children. Describe what you do at work and introduce the family to your 9 to 5 so that they can grow up understanding why it's so important and so cool that "mommy works." Third, try to seek flexibility on the job. Maybe you can work from home one or two days a week and spend more time with your kids. Eliminating the guilt will inevitably free up your financial outlook on your life and your family's life. You'll be able to better organize your priorities, including providing for the kids and for yourself. Finally, spend time, not money. Instead of going to the toy store on the weekends, spend time in the park or have your children's friends over. The important thing is to follow through on your personal goal to allocate money toward savings and give your kids the time they don't normally get with you during the week. That's a memory they'll cherish and respect, more than the $15 toy you would have bought them.

Remember, to cut the clutter you must first identify the emotional barriers that are keeping you from getting a grip on what's important to you. They could be embedded in a relationship, or perhaps you're struggling with your own personal insecurity. Next, understand that this clutter does not benefit your bottom line and how it's distracting you from leading an organized financial life. Finally, commit to eliminating the drama and returning to your priorities and goals. That leads us to the last step, practicing good habits.

Step 3. Practice Good Habits

After you've worked through Steps 1 and 2, it's time to create and follow through on certain habits that will keep you committed to an organized financial life. Here are the top six habits to secure good financial organization:

1. **Deal with it right away.** Save yourself aggravation and deal with any financial issues as they arise. When a letter from your bank arrives, don't just stick in your junk drawer. It might have helpful information, or it may be a bill. Either way, if you shrug it off, it may come back to haunt you. The ten minutes you spend sorting through mail can be a way to reinforce good, consistent behaviors toward financial organization. Whether it's a credit card statement or a messy drawer full of receipts, addressing all aspects of your financial life in a timely fashion is an effective habit that will earn you the benefit of not having to worry or feel at a loss down the road. For those who are self-employed, invoice right away upon completion of a job to ensure fast payment.

2. **Create your own deadlines.** Even the best of us are forgetful. Forgetting about your financial goals and obligations can end up being a costly slip-up. The most effective way to get people to stick to deadlines is to be, in some ways, dictatorial about it. Like, "You must pay on the fifteenth or we will shut off your water." That should be enough to get someone to pay on time. But it doesn't always work. So, one way to lessen our tendency to miss deadlines is to create our *own* deadlines—a precomittment. If your phone bill is due at the end of the month, make a point to pay it on the 25th of each month. Give yourself the wiggle room and pay early. It not only makes you

more efficient; it will give you peace of mind. Not to mention, you'll feel more in control. Duke Professor and author Dan Ariely conducted an experiment with his students in which he let one class choose their own deadlines for three papers. In another class, he told students they needed to submit the three papers by the end of the semester, with no rewards for turning in their work early. In a third class, he used a dictatorial approach and said students must submit the three papers at the fourth, eighth, and twelfth weeks of class—or else! Which class performed the best? Well, the class that received dictatorial treatment earned the highest marks. But the class that made their own deadlines showed improved grades, too. As Ariely writes, "the biggest revelation is that simply offering the students a tool by which they could precommit to deadlines helped them achieve better grades."

In your financial world, where you may have dozens of deadlines and no clear system for organizing bills and payments, you might find it helpful to set your own deadlines. For example, if your mortgage is technically due on the fifteenth of every month, set a deadline of, say, the tenth of every month to ensure you never fall behind. To reinforce the deadline, lock it into your calendar and set alarms on your phone and PDA to remind you of the approaching deadline. Or, arrange for the payment to be deducted automatically from your checking account.

Do you want to save but seem to come up dry at the end of the month? A precommitment to paying yourself first and saving automatically in your employer's 401k plan before you get your paycheck will ensure that you save well. A precommitment is extremely beneficial, Ariely says, "otherwise… we keep on falling for temptation."

You may also be able to request that your bank send e-mail alerts regarding your account balances and your savings goals. As for keeping to the organization of your goals and priorities, it's helpful to share them with others you trust so that they, too, can help you reinforce what's important to you in your life. Call it a "money buddy." My money buddy is my mom. She knows my goal is to save up for a family and house in a few years. So, if I'm obsessing over a pair of $250 shoes, she'll flat out tell me, "It's not in your plan, Farnoosh. Stick to your plan!"

3. **Stay consistent.** Associated with Step 2, setting deadlines, is staying consistent. The best way to do this is to automate as many of your financial responsibilities as possible so that you never fall behind. For example, electronically link your checking account to your mortgage collector, the town treasurer (who collects taxes), the heating company, and your healthcare provider. You never have to be unsure about when to pay bills because they'll be automatically addressed each month. As for savings, decide on a percentage of your income to be automatically deposited into a savings account bearing the highest interest rate you can find.

4. **Seek balance.** Our financial lives can easily get complicated and convoluted if we don't constantly try to get rid of the white noise. There are lots of changes you'll make to your financial life as you age and hit various milestones in life. The best thing to keep in mind is that while the ideal may be to "have it all," that doesn't mean having it all "at once." When your world becomes overwhelming, make sure you go back to the first step of cutting the clutter and eliminating stress. Physically it's also important to cut the clutter. If you have too much "stuff," too many old statements, old receipts, old forms, just shred them if you don't need them. Become comfortable with detaching yourself from the clutter. And when a new expense enters your

life, a new child or a new house, it's important to reevaluate your life to re-create financial balance. For example, if the mortgage on your new house is an extra $300 a month more than your previous home loan, how can you find that $300 from another area of your life?

5. **Keep tabs.** Behavioral experts tell me the key to getting out of bad spending habits is to track your behavior. Did you know that our messy money habits net thousands of lost dollars per year? Men are the worst at forgetting how they spent their cash. Visa USA found that men 34 and under spent close to $60 a week on things they couldn't account for, totaling more than $3,000 a year.[1] Women, meantime, lost an average $2,700 a year on miscellaneous buys. The solution is to track your spending for one week. Although some financial experts advise keeping a strict budget and writing down all that you purchase for one month to learn your spending habits, that's not at all practical. David Bach, the best-selling author of the *Finish Rich* series, tells me that seven days of tracking should be enough monitoring. "It's an honest snapshot of how you spend money," says Bach. "The key is to not change the way you spend money. Don't become a better person on the third or fourth day." In his research, Bach has found that on average many people spend 50% more a day than they actually think they're spending. Sites like Bach's AutomaticMoneyManager.com and Mint.com can help trace your spending.

In addition, ever year, quarter, month, week, and day, you can be doing some activity to ensure everything is going smoothly—that all your bills and other financial paperwork are in their place and that you're current with any updates in your financial life. Here's a checklist of smart follow-ups to make throughout the year.

Every Year

A new year offers a new beginning, a chance to set a fresh personal finance agenda and to end the bad behaviors of the past year. Start with getting your free credit report. You are entitled to one from each of the three major credit reporting bureaus: Experian, TransUnion, and Equifax. My preference is to download a free copy from one and stagger the other two through the year to track my progress. All are available for free through AnnualCreditReport.com. Also, in early January, start collecting your tax statements from the various entities that paid you in the previous year and agencies to which you paid taxes. You'll know from the envelopes because they'll usually say "Important Tax Forms Enclosed." Expect mail from your employer, your student loan organization, your municipality (if you paid real estate taxes), and maybe even your bank, plus any other firms where you have investments (if you earned interest on any savings). In early February or March (depending on how soon you want to start filing your taxes), start logging all your itemized expenses into a spreadsheet or some sort of accessible software to help you as you prepare your taxes in April. In December, make sure you've received all the receipts from the various charities to which you donated throughout the year. These will come in handy for the next tax-filing season since some donations are tax deductible!

Every Quarter

You want to review your investment statements—from your 401k to your IRA, child's 529 plan, and stock portfolio—at least once every quarter to make sure you are staying balanced and diversified. Every quarter you also want to schedule a time to recap your goals with your partner or spouse, to make sure you're on the right path and schedule to financially afford your goals. This is a good time to bring up any concerns, and it's best to do it when you're both in a good mood. Schedule a time when you can both comfortably recap the last three months.

Every Month

Every 30 days, you want to review your billing statements for credit cards and other monthly expenses like cable, phone, and utilities. Make sure you haven't been charged erroneously.

Every Week

Empty out your wallet and dump out receipts older than 45 days. Unless the store has a limit-free returns policy, you probably don't need this receipt anymore, and your wallet is just carrying extra cargo. Cut this clutter out of your life! (One exception: warranty receipts. Keep them for the life of the warranty.)

Every Day

Just like you may step on a scale each day to check your weight and remind yourself why you shouldn't have that piece of pie after dinner, check your bank balance each day to remind yourself of where you stand financially. Knowing you have, say, $800 left in checking with two weeks left to go in the month may, or may not, give you the assurance to eat out a couple nights this week, depending on how much of your obligations have been accounted for at that point. In other words, are your bases covered? If the mortgage and car payments have already been paid and the credit card bill has been paid, you may figure that a couple nights out on the town won't break the bank. But it always helps to double check, daily! At the end of the day, I like to empty out my change purse and dump any and all loose change into a mason jar on my desk. It's just a habit that has kept me conscious and consistent with savings. Of course, I do have other savings tools, like CDs and money market accounts, but a coin jar is a nice added bonus that's a visual reminder of the importance to save. A few more months of coin collecting and my daily habit could translate into dinner and a movie. Okay, maybe just dinner. But still!

6. **Create personal rules of thumb.** As Jay Ritter, the Cordell professor of finance at the University of Florida, tells me, humans are creatures of habit. We thrive when we have rules of thumb ways to guide us. Like your money philosophies, you need to devise rules of thumb that offer parameters and speak to your personal organization needs and goals. It's best to start with your biggest problem areas. If you are having difficulty paying your bills on time, a rule of thumb that might work is this: "I pay my bills every first Monday of the month." If you tend to lose receipts and get burned when trying to return things, create a rule of thumb for yourself like this: "I always keep my receipts for 45 days in this box." The same helps with dieting, says Ritter. If your weakness is midnight snacking, for example, committing to a parameter like "I don't eat after 8 p.m." may make it easier to avoid the fridge.

Let's Get Physical!

Now that you understand the psychological underpinnings of sound financial practices, let's look at your physical surroundings. I know you've been dying to discuss color-coordinated storage folders for all your paperwork, haven't you? Good. So have I. But not all your finances are best-managed offline. There are fabulous online resources to help guide you through the maze of money. Let's start there.

Online Assistance

Budgeting tools. Free personal finance software sites like Mint.com, Wesabe.com, and Thrive.com offer a way to manage many of our financial accounts, from savings and checking to our home mortgage and credit cards.

Spending trackers. Various smart phone applications can help us better track our expenses. If you like having mobile access to your spending records, there are applications you can download from iTunes for $1 to $5. The most popular ones are BillTracker, AceBudget, iExpenseIt, and Xpense Tracker.

Free bank help. Your bank will likely have a variety of online and mobile services to keep your finances organized. For example, Bank of America customers can receive free text alerts regarding their bank account balances. Online, you can also track your spending by reviewing debit and credit card purchases.

Offline Assistance

Receipt box. Because I freelance and have my own business, it's important that I keep a record of all my work-related expenses, from travel to stationary to office equipment and transportation, for tax purposes. In February, I usually dump this box out and start logging my expenses to guide me through my tax filing in April.

Storage for paper trails. I have two accordion folders purchased from Staples ($12.99 each), one for my taxes and one for everything else. The one for my taxes includes the past three years of statements and returns, because that's usually the longest the IRS waits to audit you. In the other folder, I have the following categories of paperwork: mortgage, deed to home, utility statements, insurance (health and home), investment statements, agency contracts, warranties, employment records, cable, and pay stubs.

Safety box. Your passport, birth certificate, and any other hard-to-replace valuables should be stored in a fire-proof safety lock box in your home.

Shredder. A shredder represents your best protection against identity theft. In my kitchen, I have a basket into which all my junk mail travels. At the end of each week, I open up those envelopes and shred all the documents that include my personal information.

Goal-supportive visuals. It's not cheesy to put your goals in visual perspective. Creating a colorful board of images, magazine cutouts, photographs, and so on depicting your future goals is a great investment of your time, as it will serve as a constant reminder and reinforcement of what your "good life" is all about. Place the board somewhere you'll notice it daily. You can also create screen savers on your computer to visualize a goal. Right now on my MacBook, I have a lovely photo of the Eiffel Tower, symbolic of my goal to return to Paris for vacation in the next year or two.

Security account. You want to have a hardcopy list of all your usernames and passwords for your various online accounts (for example, frequent flier programs, banks, credit card companies, cable company, utilities, and health insurer). So that you have a backup, e-mail the list to your personal e-mail account and file it there. Don't leave it on your hard drive, in case your computer or laptop gets hacked into.

Remember, the key to an organized life (and one that's moving forward)—whether it relates to your finances, your relationships, or career—is to maintain your composure and not get overwhelmed. To remain on top of your financial plan, revisit your goals, clear the clutter, and stick to good habits. Consistency really pays off in this department.

---

[1] Visa USA Survey, 2007.

6

Be Your Biggest Advocate

"Insist upon yourself."

Ralph Waldo Emerson

I absolutely love to hear stories about people negotiating their way to better interest rates, reduced fees, and getting their money back. (Is that weird?) On *Bank of Mom & Dad,* I worked with a young woman and helped her convince her bank to lower the interest rate on a credit card, which ultimately helped reduce her minimum monthly payments from $1,800 a month to $400 a month. We ran the math and found that if she continued to pay $1,800 a month with the new lower interest rate, she'd be out of debt in less than 5 years, versus 30. It was so incredible a moment, she nearly cried in disbelief. Even I was shocked by how much the bank helped. And no, it wasn't because it was for a TV show. The bank actually had a special program for struggling borrowers that we only learned about once she called asking for help. I call this being your own advocate.

Being an advocate for yourself is critically important because no person or institution cares more about your money than you. That's not just my personal philosophy. That's a proven fact. That's why there's 8-point font on the back of credit card statements. That's why retailers aren't always upfront about their return policies and why there are more than 27 million victims of identity fraud in this country. Banks don't give you a courtesy call to say when you're close to running on empty. Instead, they hope you go over your limit so that they can rack up overdraft fees. Fees and other noninterest income made up nearly $40 billion in bank revenues in 2009,[1] and according to the *New York Times*, the average customer paid a dozen overdraft or insufficient-fund charges that same year, at $30 a ding.[2]

Fortunately, current law requires financial institutions to be clearer and more transparent about their rules and regulations. The Credit Card Act of 2009 prohibits credit card companies from jacking up interest rates without fair warning. And if you're a card holder with a consistent history of paying on time, your rate cannot increase on any outstanding balance, unless your rate was a "teaser" (i.e., promotional) rate or unless you hold a variable rate credit card. And those pesky overdraft fees? Since July 2010, banks are also required to get permission from customers before letting their debit card transactions go through when there isn't enough money in the account to cover the charge.

I mentioned a few new regulations that favor consumers, but banks still continue to find ways to impose fees. We still live in a world of *them* against us. Them being the financial institutions, the retailers, even sometimes our friends and family who tug away at our purse strings and try to get access to our hard-earned money. If we are conscious about this and take the role of advocate, we can better reclaim control of our money. Unless we speak up and make some behavioral changes, no one is going to volunteer to help us out. And worse, we risk losing our financial bearings and we risk not accomplishing our goals.

The Art of Personal Advocacy

True financial advocacy requires self-determination and self-awareness. The average person often remains on the sidelines even when getting into the game means the chance for a better deal or rate. We come up with excuses to avoid change and thus reinforce the status quo. Professor Jay Ritter explains that "people make decisions once, and unless there's a strong reason to change things, that's where they tend to remain." He calls it lethargy. I call it lazy. Banks, credit card companies, and cable and cell phone companies actually depend on our lazy butts, hoping we'll go years without changing what we signed up for.

Combating lethargy and being an active advocate means six things:

1. Being committed
2. Knowing your rights
3. Exercising common sense
4. Having persistence
5. Identifying helpful resources
6. And always, always, assuming there are risks to everything

The Composite of Self-Advocate

Here's more on what an effective self-advocate looks like:

> **Self-determination.** Having self-determination in the context of your financial life basically means having the freedom to be in charge of financial decisions. If you depend on someone else's financial means, it is difficult to be an advocate for your financial well-being. That's why it's important that you do what it takes to earn your own money, even if you're a stay-at-home mom. And if you are in a single-income household, take responsibility for the organization and bill paying so that you have a current and working knowledge of your household finances. Never be in the dark. And, agree with your partner that even though there's just one income, both of you have the power and vested interest to be advocates for your family's money.

Self-awareness. Awareness of your history—from a credit and purchasing perspective—can greatly enhance your ability to be a financial self-advocate. For example, a clean bill of credit and a high credit score (for example, higher than 740) will, in most cases, earn you the best interest rate on a bank loan. Knowing this, you advocate for yourself during a loan application process, in case the bank returns with a higher-than-expected rate. In contrast, if you have a bad credit report and you're up for a job where your credit is being checked, the employer may perceive this as a red flag. By knowing your track record, you can be an advocate for yourself. Be upfront and clear about how your credit got tarnished and specifically what you are doing to clean up the mess. Maybe your credit took a hit because of a divorce or health-related expenses. Many employers will respect that you are working to improve your situation.

Know your rights. Understand what you are legally entitled to, whether it is a plane ticket that you purchased from Expedia, a municipal bond you bought through your brokerage, or flowers you ordered from the Internet. You need to understand all the terms and conditions (including risks).

Exercise common sense. Exercising common sense is all about being realistic and boiling things down to a "let me get this straight" place. Legal jargon and fine print aside, do you feel you're being taken advantage of in some way? Can you articulate this in a way so that the person at the other end of the line or across the counter can empathize and enforce (or maybe even bend) the rules for you?

My Story:
What Being an Advocate Looks Like

My parents recently rented a van from Enterprise Rent-a-Car to help move my brother to college (from San Francisco to Irvine, California, about 400 miles away). About an hour before they arrived in Irvine, the van broke down on a Los Angeles freeway (in the middle of the night!). A tow truck took them and the broken-down vehicle to the nearest Enterprise office at LAX airport. Enterprise employees at that facility told my family that because they had rented the car from an independently owned and operate Enterprise location in San Francisco, their rental records were not showing up in the system at LAX. Contractually, this LAX office was not obligated to help my parents get a new van free of charge or help them in any other way.

Here is how you get to the bottom line: So, let me see whether I understand this correctly (say this with a smile, always): I rented a car from a company bearing your same name (even though it is not the same operator), the car dies on us in the middle of the freeway where we could have gotten run over, and now you are telling me that there's nothing, absolutely nothing you can do? Believe me, we would go back and deal with this problem in San Francisco, but that's about 400 miles away. It's midnight, and my son needs to check into his dorm tomorrow. What's our alternative?

> *Suddenly, common sense kicks in and the attendant realizes the company's rules are not humanely applicable in this situation. Apparently, there was something she could do, and at that moment she was convinced enough to take action. She handed my parents the keys to a new van and booked them a hotel room at the nearby Marriot where they could rest overnight and continue their drive in the morning. As for the old broken-down van? "We'll send that up to San Francisco in the morning for an inspection; no worries," she told my parents.*

Be persistent. Persistence pays. Check your bank statements at least once a month, check mortgage rates every week, and always read the fine print on everything. These are all persistent behaviors of a money advocate and can help you save money.

Reference helpful resources. Ideally, you want to handle the situation yourself, without involving other advocates. But it's worth identifying resources that can support your claim or cause, because sometimes it helps to have backup. Here are a few to consider:

If you're in debt, one great advocacy partner is the National Foundation for Credit Counseling (www.nfcc.org), a nonprofit that connects people who are in debt or have other financial problems with credit counselors in their area.

The Better Business Bureau (www.bbb.org, and enter your ZIP code for the bureau nearest you) is a great resource if you want some additional help when battling with a local business. The mere threat to contact the BBB is sometimes enough to get owners to cooperate, since a negative review from the BBB can sometimes really hurt a business.

Be aware of risks. There's no such thing as risk free. We need to think of all the possible outcomes before committing to any financial decision. We already understand that investing in the stock market has its risks. But there's more. Not to frighten you, but there is also a risk (albeit a smaller one) in opening a bank account, donating to a charity, working with a financial consultant, renting a house, and in some cases, even paying off your mortgage too quickly.

Assume accountability. To be a great personal advocate, you need to remain accountable for all your financial responsibilities and goals. Yes, banks and consumer laws promise us certain protections, but accountability is a two-way street, and many of us (as evidenced by the personal financial losses in the recession) have not been as active in this lane. As a society, we fell out of touch with this very important behavior during the boom years before the recent recession.

I appeared on the *Today Show* to discuss then-presidential hopeful John McCain's explanation to voters as to the cause of the financial collapse in 2008. It was simply "Wall Street greed," he explained. "Is he right?" Matt Lauer asked me. Well, I replied, if he was talking to an audience of 5-year-olds, McCain's answer might be acceptable. After all, children don't quite yet understand the complexities of the world we live in. Sure, greed is to blame, but there's much more to this recession than a bunch of white-collar bad guys. What about those consumers who signed on to risky mortgages with adjustable rates that they knew would adjust higher and so face potentially higher monthly bills? And those who purchased homes wildly out of their league? At the end of the day, whose fault is it when we spend more than we earn? I'm no political theorist, but I suppose telling prospective voters that they were partly to blame for the stock market and housing market calamities was too risky a move. But the grave reality is that consumers share the blame with those fat cat bankers for not assuming accountability for their financial decisions.

Some people emerged from the recession relatively unscathed. These individuals put their money to work (safely). They didn't wait for their financial planner to call the shots. People like my tax accountant, for example, who boasted at our last meeting that his retirement account actually earned 3% in 2008 while most 401k accounts tumbled by 40%. It wasn't his best year, but he is just thankful he didn't lose money like the majority of investors. "How did you see it coming?" I asked. "I'm 60 years old. I've seen it all before, and I can tell when a market's about to collapse. The signs were all there. There was too much exuberance, and our portfolio had earned double-digit percentage gains for the last five years straight. So, a year before the stock market crashed, when signs were pointing toward a bursting bubble, we put most of our retirement money in bonds and the money market." That smart and rational preemptive strike helped preserve their savings.

To lower financial risk, you need to be aware of all details of your current financial involvements. When calling a credit card company to ask for a lower rate, you don't want to be caught off guard when the agent tells you that you are ineligible because of recent missed payments. Read all the fine print, stay organized, and don't be afraid or embarrassed to get answers to your questions from your bank, your credit card company, and anywhere else you involve your money. These are all the top attributes of strong accountants. Along the way, it also helps to stay accountable and have a "money buddy" or a support group.

More on Accountability

As a sidebar to staying accountable, here is a list of professionals who can help you better understand and manage your various financial accounts. I don't want to send the message that trusting professionals is dangerous. On the contrary, getting the right help is critical in some cases. But because you want to assume accountability, you don't want to blindly trust these people can do it all (and without failure). The following paragraphs identify what you need to know about the limits of each professional's services.

Your bank rep. The cost is free to enlist the help of this person. You can expect him to help you open a new savings or checking account, explain confusing fees, transfer money to various funds you hold at the bank, cut you a break on an overdraft fee (if you're convincing!), update you on new offers with better interest rates within the bank, and explain how your account is affected in the event of a bank merger or bankruptcy. A bank rep won't tell you tell you if you can get a better interest rate elsewhere or whether you can truly "afford" a loan.

Your 401k plan administrator. If you are enrolled in a 401k plan offered through your employer, the plan administrator is at your service for free. He or she will help craft a retirement portfolio based on your risk tolerance and time horizon, update you on your account balance and investment options, explain any taxes and penalties if you withdraw money, plus any other fees, and walk you through your statements and help you roll your account over if you leave your job. This person cannot guarantee that your investments won't depreciate or tip you off that the market is crashing.

Your accountant. The cost of hiring an accountant depends on how complex your taxes are. If you are an individual (not a small business), the cost will be about $400 for a basic return, approximately $200 for two hours. Your accountant will file your annual tax returns, help reduce your taxable income by deducting allowable expenses, advise you on paperwork to keep (and for how long), and advise you about how changes in income (job loss, inheritance, business start-ups) may affect your taxes.

He won't tell you that you're paying for some work that you could actually do yourself, such as organizing receipts and paperwork and itemizing deductions. Chances are, he won't store any of your receipts for you, either. You'll have to organize that for yourself. Accountants also won't just offer their personal background check for your reassurance. Sure, the diploma's on the wall, but what about previous experience? Choose wisely by partnering with a certified public accountant with at least five years' experience. Do a background check and double-check credentials. Ask whether any clients were audited in the past five years and how it went. Ask for certified board or association memberships. Finally, copy everything for yourself.

Your financial adviser. The cost of hiring a financial adviser runs the gamut. Some charge by the hour, whereas others require a retainer fee. Still others earn their income by taking a percentage of your portfolio. Typically, a certified financial adviser will help you construct and manage a financial portfolio, including investments, insurance, your will, college savings, and retirement, and will normally give you a free first meeting.

And remember, your financial adviser can't read your mind. You have to speak up and say if you're not comfortable with certain investments or if you have new financial goals. Also, financial advisers don't guarantee investment returns. Your financial adviser might have an MBA and be a certified financial analyst, but don't assume that he or she can guess where the market is headed any better than you can. Financial advisers also can't help you budget. That's up to you. They can diversify your investment accounts, but your personal day-to-day finances are your responsibility to manage. Stay accountable by choosing a fee-based adviser, not one who earns commissions on your business. Fees can be hourly (starting at around $150/hour), a flat rate, or a percentage of your assets under management. Interview several financial advisers before signing with any one in particular. It's a chance for you to ask a zillion questions to see whether a person is a good fit. Consider interviewing a CFA in your area through the National Association of Personal Financial Advisers (NAPFA) or the Financial Planning Association (FPA).

Your health insurance agent. The cost is free under your health insurance plan. Agents will explain medical bills and your insurance policy. They'll answer questions about what a procedure costs and what your policy covers for doctor visits, emergency room care, prescriptions, and out-of-hospital care. Expect them to also explain your flex spending or health saving accounts and tell you how much of your annual benefits are left and which doctors are in your network. What an agent won't be able to provide is availability 24 hours a day, which can be annoying during emergencies. They also cannot resolve every issue, and you might need to get your doctor or healthcare agent involved in a bill dispute.

My Story: 360° Financial Advocacy

I worked with a woman named Amy, whom I met during a financial counseling session in 2008. In the midst of a divorce, the 29-year-old was struggling with unpaid bills, an underwater mortgage, overdue credit card bills, and worst of all, no job! After seven months of marriage, things started to crumble between her and her then-husband. Feeling dejected, she came to me asking for financial help.

My goal was to gather as much information as I could about her financial records, her goals, and her personality so that I could devise a way to get her back on track. I learned that over the course of a couple years, she had racked up close to $44,000 in credit card debt (debt she was planning to pay down with her husband's income). She was currently unemployed and didn't know how to start making a dent in these obligations. In addition, she owned a home in Florida with a mortgage that was worth more than the home was currently then worth on the market. In a few months, the divorce settlement (and about $17,000) would arrive, but Amy's financial drama would continue to haunt her, unless she learned how to help herself and be her own advocate.

Amy's financial mess was a combination of her own poor decision making and the strains inherent in the recession. She also believed her ex to be a culprit, the "jerk" who let her spend freely and now refused to pay her credit card bills (charges she made during the marriage).

I explained to Amy that she could point fingers all she wanted, but the reality was that this financial debacle was all hers. I laid out her two choices: She could own up to the situation or she could waste time feeling sorry for herself and hope to get bailed out (the latter not a reality).

Amy had to accept that she is the only one in the world who cares about her financial life. Her parents love her, but they're not going to pay off her debt. Her husband said he loved her, and we know how that turned out. No husband, no parent, no bank, no broker, no divorce attorney is ever going to give a you-know-what about her money. Our meeting motivated Amy to take control of the situation. After all, she was only 29. She had her whole life ahead of her. Relatively speaking, she could have it a lot worse.

She promptly moved in with her parents for several months (a tough decision, but a rational one) to save money. Next, she began phoning her credit card companies and asking for settlements. She articulated over the phone that she was currently out of a job and desperately needed to pay down her debt, but that the current finance charges were preventing her from reducing the principal on her balances. It took some time on the phone, but Amy was able to settle her debt by paying less than 50% of the current balances. This would hurt her credit score, but for Amy, the more important thing was cleaning the slate and getting the collection agents off her back.

With her divorce settlement, she would be able to pay off these settlements in full and quickly. By taking the initiative and convincing her creditors to help resolve her debt, Amy had opened a new chapter in her life. A few months later, I followed up with Amy and learned that she was is in talks with an attorney to help get her own small business off the ground. Later, I learned she did get her event planning firm, Lucia Paul Design, up and running (and has subsequently won numerous clients and awards). She's so empowered she wants to help other young women in her community become more financially savvy. It wasn't easy, but the fact that she resolved her debt on her own made her feel in control (which is what you always want to be when it comes to your money).

Sweat the Small Stuff

Part of being a powerful self-advocate is to know which battles are worth fighting. And you might be surprised to discover how the little things can really add up. Here's a list of everyday expenses we can potentially lower by being advocates:

Your home insurance. The latest figures from the Insurance Information Institute show the average homeowner's insurance premium is about $700 a year. Play advocate by calling your insurance provider and asking about every available discount. If you don't immediately qualify, mention any improvements you've made to the home. If you upgraded plumbing or electrical, added a security system, smoke detectors, and so on, all that can shave 10% to 20% off your premium. A phone call to your insurance company could save you more than $100 annually.

Your car insurance. The average cost for auto insurance in the United States is roughly $800 per year. You might be able to save a bit on that, though. For instance, perhaps you work from home now and drive less, or maybe you're taking public transportation more often, or bought a safer car, or took the keys away from your teenager. In these scenarios, it's definitely worth your time to call your car insurance company and let them know about any changes that may affect your premium rate. Some changes lower your risk as a client, and so they won't charge as much to insure you as they did before. If you can shave off even just 15% because you are using your car less, that's a $120 savings with just one phone call.

Your cell phone bill. Ask about friends and family deals. The term *friends and family* has become loosely defined over the years, and some carriers will accept a roommate or your third cousin removed as a "friend or family" member. You basically share a plan and make calls to each other for free. For two people on a shared plan, the monthly cost may be only $50 rather than $80 when you pay for each line separately. In a year, that's $360 savings.

Tuition. Experts at FinAid.org, a financial aid website for college students, say that if you have had any changes to your financial situation in the past year (e.g., job loss/cutback), you should call to ask about getting extra financial aid from your or your child's university. If you have less money coming in than a year ago, or even six months ago, you should call the school's financial aid office and ask for what's called a "professional judgment review," in which the school reassesses (factoring in your new circumstances) your need for financial aid. They'll want documents, a copy of your layoff notice, and a list of circumstances that have changed. The savings? Potentially thousands of dollars. More than 90% of colleges responding to a 2009 survey by the National Association of Independent Colleges and Universities said they were increasing their financial aid budgets. Michigan State University, where students were hit hardest by the collapse of the auto industry, set up a $500,000 fund for financially troubled families. A financial aid spokesperson at Michigan State told me they awarded needy students anywhere from $900 to $7,000 per student, but it was ultimately up to the students and parents to speak up and ask for help. If you find yourself in a financial bind, FinAid.org says you can potentially get an additional $2,000 to $5,000 in financial aid by seeking a review of your application.

Your cable, TV, and Internet bills. New deals and sign-up incentives are always around for new customers, but even if you're an existing customer, call and ask whether you qualify for these new deals. If not, mention that you are considering canceling your premium channels. That usually earns you a discount. Bring up a better offer, and say you plan to switch. They'll likely make some concessions. Ask about any triple-play bundles of TV, Internet, and voice service. If you're already paying for all three separately, perhaps you can save money by bundling them into one deal.

If it doesn't work, ask one more time, politely. The key here is let them know you've been a long-standing customer. This way, you're in a good place to negotiate and ask for some wiggle room. The last-ditch effort is to simply threaten to cancel. Discounts vary from provider to region to each individual customer, but expect at least $10 off your monthly bill for six months. That's $60 right away. If you have an even more expensive plan, you can save as much as $20 per month for over six months. That's up to $120 total for the year.

Being your own financial advocate means standing up for your rights and protecting your money. Once you embrace this, you are ready to discover the ways to make the kind of personal financial decisions that will reap dividends now and in the future, the money choices that are truly worth it (to you).

[1] 2009 Moebs Services Survey.

[2] Ron Lieber, "Free Checking Could Go the Way of Free Toasters," *New York Times,* January 22, 2010.

7

Make Your Money Count

"Try not to become a man of success, but rather try to become a man of value."

Albert Einstein

As Einstein saw it, pursuing a life of value is the greatest goal. A life of value has more to offer you and the world around you than a life of success. After all, a life of value keeps on giving. It inspires and teaches, offers happiness, and ultimately leaves a legacy.

This chapter explains how to pursue a financial life with an emphasis on value, how to make the most of your money in a way that reaps dividends down the road, and have it ultimately live up to be a sound and wise investment. In short, how to make financial moves that we can proudly say are "worth it." Just because something is affordable doesn't make it *worthy*.

I've examined this from several angles—both from my own experiences and that of others—and in this chapter, you'll find a formula for determining what a worthy expense looks like, no matter how big or small the financial move. The formula is broken down into the following critical factors:

Comfortable affordability. After weighing all of your finances, you are confident and secure in paying for this particular item or event, whether it means paying for it all in cash or via a loan.

Good utility. The financial move should have satisfying purpose and benefits, financially, psychologically, or both. What are you receiving in exchange for your money? What's the *quality* of the return?

Manageable risks. Examine the potential drawbacks of the financial move and how well you're prepared and able to deal with them. What will this purchase cost you *in practice*. And what if things don't go as you presume? In other words, what are the *opportunity costs?* For instance, how will spending $50,000 on a wedding affect the first few years of your marriage? A financial move that's worth it may have risks, but they are *manageable*—meaning you are ready, willing, and able to handle the potential downside.

If you discover that you're financially and emotionally confident in all of these three areas, don't be held back. Whether it's starting a business, going back to school, buying property, throwing a huge wedding, or so forth, chances are it's worth it to you if all these variables are answered in the positive.

What "Worthy" Looks Like

"Worthy" can be an extremely relative point of view. We may be biased as to the meaning of *worthy* based on past experiences, our goals, and our ability to spend. Let's take that out of the equation and examine the notion of *worth* as objectively as possible. A few key areas need to be examined, beginning with an understanding of affordable versus unaffordable.

Affordable vs. Unaffordable

When you are considering the affordability of an item or event, it's important to see whether your top bases are covered. Remember the bases from the first chapter, the obligations we need to fulfill to go on to achieve our version of rich? The most important ones include sufficient earnings, a variety of savings (rainy day and retirement), and no revolving debt. Have you addressed these? That's a good first question to ask when considering whether you can afford a specific financial decision. Someone *without* a stated money plan, in contrast, might make the purchase by tapping into an emergency nest egg, stretching the monthly paycheck, or paying thousands in interest over the next few years by using a credit card (and all the while without putting any money aside for retirement).

From there, look at how readily and easily you can afford the purchase. If the money is sitting in your bank account, you're a step ahead of the game. But purchasing it with a credit card may just get you into a debt trap—and works against the affordability of the expense. A bank loan can be equally troubling. Although you don't have the complications of accruing credit card debt, you do have to pay the loan. And those monthly payments may have to come out of your savings plan.

What constitutes unaffordable? If you find yourself carrying revolving debt to purchase discretionary items, you may be living way beyond your means and need to reevaluate your goals and your budget. Squeezing in more purchases that'll only add to your debt is an unaffordable move. It may be more appropriate to use revolving credit to pay for large-ticket items and stretch out those payments. For purchases of $1,000 or less, however, it makes more sense to use cash rather than credit, given all the interest you'll be paying.

For years I've been saying that cash helps us save because it has real financial limitations as compared to a credit card. Once the cash is gone, you can't spend anymore. Credit cards give people a false license to shop above their means. In fact, credit experts, including Gerri Detweiler of Credit.com and Gail Cunningham of the National

Foundation for Credit Counseling, tell me that credit cards lead us to overspend by 20%.

But my perspective runs much deeper: You should use cash not only because it's practical, but because it's the *right* thing to do. Economist Dan Ariely's research finds that "cash keeps us honest." By using cash instead of credit, we will be prompted to make smarter purchasing decisions that more closely match our actual needs. Credit cards cue people to make rash purchasing choices and spend more than they have, simply because they can. "When we deal with cash, we are primed to think about our actions as if we had just signed an honor code," Dan tells me.

Easier said than done, I realize. We struggle to pay with cash because it's painful, Dan tells me. In economic terms, he calls this the "pain of pain." He tells me to imagine going to a nice meal and at the end of the dinner paying with either a credit card or cash. Which feels better? For most people, it's paying with a credit card. Why? "When the timing of consumption and spending coincide, we enjoy the experience less," he says. For this reason, we also gravitate to unlimited monthly deals and bill-me-later options—even it means we end up paying more than we would if we opted for a pay-as-you-go plan.

"If you want to save money, you should opt to do things that have more 'pain of pain,'" suggests Dan. And as it happens, today consumers are opting for the "pain of pain" plan, as evidenced by Visa's latest earnings report in which the company said more consumers are making debit transactions (i.e., using cash in their checking accounts) instead of relying on credit.[1]

I asked Dan if there was a cheerier name for this strategy, but he just laughed. Bottom line, he advised, you want to choose financial options that make you much more conscious of your money, especially if saving is a priority. According to Dan, "If you want to give it a good name, say that you want to make more thoughtful decisions… be deliberative."

Pursuing a Credit-Free Life

Although it's not advised that you ditch the use of credit cards entirely (after all, you need them to help establish credit so that you can later qualify for a mortgage, a car loan, a personal loan, or even a job in some cases), it is possible to live mainly off your hard-earned cash. Some may want to pursue this plan because they want to stay on a strict budget and don't trust themselves with credit cards. For others, the purpose is to help get out of existing credit card debt. Here are my top tips for living credit free:

Build savings. Credit cards are often used in emergency situations, when your car breaks down, a water leak leaves your basement flooded, or you need to quickly book a flight. But if you want to live credit free, you must rely on your savings in such situations. To do this, it's imperative that you have a healthy amount of savings. Stay as liquid as possible. A savings cushion linked to a different debit card or checkbook may be one helpful solution.

Keep constant tabs on your money. This is something everyone should do no matter what. We talked about this in the chapter on staying organized. And for those who opt for a cash-based existence, getting e-mail or text alerts from your bank with your daily balance is especially helpful, as is signing up online for a free personal finance software that can help you track spending.

Connect checking with savings. As a further step to reduce the chances of bounced check or insufficient fund fees, link your checking and savings accounts at your bank. This way, if there's a shortfall in your checking account next time you swipe your debit card at the store, the money in your savings account can cover the gap. This is usually a free service, although in some cases banks may charge a small transfer fee for linked accounts.

Keep credit cards open and active *enough*. Although it might seem logical and even cathartic to close an old credit card account, doing so may end up damaging your credit score. Your credit score, as determined by Fair Isaac Corporation (FICO), factors in heavily your credit history and the amount of credit in your name. The longer the history and the more credit you have, the better. Closing an account will wipe out the history of that card and erase that line of credit in your name, which may knock points off your credit score. Gail Cunningham, my trusted source at the National Foundation of Credit Counselors, suggests keeping your existing credit card accounts "active" by charging a small amount to them each month for, say, only fixed expenses, like cable or car insurance, and linking those cards to a checking account that pays off the balances in full automatically each month.

The Credit Card Accountability Responsibility and Disclosure Act of 2009 (effective early 2010), enacted by the federal government to benefit cardholders, says consumers must opt-in for overdraft service. In the past, overdraft services had just been provided by banks (at their discretion) and marketed as a "benefit" to consumers who went over an account's limit. Instead of rejecting the transaction, the bank would approve it, despite insufficient funds. It saved the consumer some embarrassment, but the fee for overdraft protection could be up to $35 each time. By connecting checking with savings, you may not need to opt-in for this service and you may save a great deal of money.

Measuring Utility

Once you've come to the confident conclusion that a purchase is affordable—the math works and your bases are covered—you need to identify the use and benefits of the purchase. *Utility* is a measure of the purpose and benefits of a particular financial decision.

Something with great utility is reassuring because we feel we're making the most of our money, exchanging it for something that will offer a great return either financially or psychologically or, in the best-case scenario, both. Like, *the market's rocky right now but buying this beach house today at a discounted price will prove to be a great investment down the road, and it's comforting to know I can retire here someday. It's worth it.* Or, *getting my MBA will take me two years and $100,000 in student loans to complete the degree, but given that I'll probably be able to increase my rank and salary by 50% right after school, it'll totally be worth it.*

Understanding utility can help us justify (or not) expensive financial decisions. When you attach high value to a purchase or financial move, there's less chance of having buyer's remorse, and you are more inclined to maintain it and perhaps even build more value in to it (like the beach house).

But determining utility can be tricky. Behaviorally, people tend to mistake high price and fancy marketing for quality and utility. Studies show that when we pay *more* for something, it makes us feel better, and we in turn think that the item is *necessarily* better. A recent study by researchers at California Institute for Technology found that when presented with two identical wines, people preferred the taste of the more expensive wine.[2]

Also, people are more likely to make irrational purchasing decisions when they're in a hurry or feel pressured. That's why infomercials make so much money. A study by *Consumer Reports* recently concluded that there's a science behind infomercials that creates brain waves that compel us to buy.[3] In fact, infomercials are perfectly written and produced to excite the dopamine levels (i.e., happiness levels) in the brain. After the loud and insisting commercials end, our dopamine levels typically drop within five to six minutes, but of course, we're encouraged to *buy now*... and often we do. Infomercials are a $150 billion industry.[4]

All this behavioral data raises these questions: How do we properly measure something's utility and value without being clouded by our brain? How can we be more in control of our money decisions? I find that the following three techniques work best:

Globalize your scope of relatively. Take the time to understand and measure how this purchase compares not just to other similar options on the market but also to everything else in your life. We tend to measure things in small relative parameters, which can muddy our perspective on whether something is really worthy. In Dan's book, he uses the example of how we might have no problem spending $3,000 to upgrade to leather seating for a car we're buying for $25,000. It seems like a small amount to spend relative to the $25,000. What's another 10%, right? But funny enough, we hesitate to spend that same $3,000 on a new sofa, despite the fact that it may offer more utility.[5] The trick here is to think about how else you spend your money, and that way you'll be better able to draw a conclusion as to the relative value, worth, and utility of a particular purchase.

Narrow your options. It's a proven behavioral fact that too many options that run the gamut causes confusion, whether items on a menu or mutual funds for your 401k. One way to deal with this phenomenon is to identify a price range you're comfortable with and stick to it. When debating what kind of a car to buy, and you know you want to spend only $28,000 to $30,000 soup to nuts, stick to reviewing a few vehicles in that price range. Don't cross the $30,000 threshold. Stick to your guns. When you look at cars that cost more than $30,000, temptation kicks in and you may try to justify spending more than initially planned.

It's no coincidence that Greg Rapp, a restaurant menu engineer, sometimes puts an outrageously expensive item on the menu. He does this to cause patrons to think that the less-expensive (although still pricey) menu items are a better value. I first learned about Rapp during a segment on the *Today Show* in which I gave advice about how to save money when eating out. Rapp was introduced in the first half of the segment as a sort of "menu psychologist" who helped restaurant owners increase profits by manipulating their menu design and layout.

Detach. Remember what you learned earlier in this chapter about making financial decisions under time pressure, such as when viewing an infomercial? Here's a way to counter this behavioral trait. Take a breather. Give yourself at least 10 minutes to disassociate your brain from the commercial's or salesperson's fanfare. You'll be able to make a better decision after your dopamine levels calm down. Chances are, without the sense of urgency or all the pressure around you to buy, you can make a sounder decision and you won't feel that you missed an opportunity if you skip it.

Mitigating Risks

After you determine the affordability and utility of the purchase, you then need to examine the *effects* of this financial move. Will it compromise your comfort level in life? Does this purchase make sense in a financial and *personal* way? What risks and compromises might you need to make to fulfill this purchase? What are the opportunity costs?

Measuring drawbacks can be somewhat subjective. For example, you're not going to get everyone to agree that going back to school for a higher degree is necessarily purposeful or beneficial. It depends on the degree, it depends on the likelihood you'll find a higher-paying job, and it depends on *you*. The thought of a six-figure loan is enough for many to shy away from quitting a paid job and going back to school. It may be too big of a risk not knowing whether you'll have a job available when you graduate. For others, however, no matter the debt load, they may be willing to go back to school because they consider it an investment in themselves that will reap rewards, both tangible and intangible, down the road.

The last piece of this analysis is meant to determine your capacity to handle your appetite for risk. For example, you might have enough now to buy a new house and you're convinced it will offer great financial benefits, but is it something you can truly afford with potential layoffs happening at your company? Do you have a Plan B in case things go awry?

Investing in Yourself

Investing in yourself is one of the most *worthwhile* things you can do. As Ralph Waldo Emerson said, *"Make the most of yourself, for that is all there is of you."* To invest in yourself is to invest in the activities, relationships, and challenges that will pay off not just financially but also psychologically. From joining the gym to traveling the world, starting a side business to taking extra courses, to moving to a neighborhood with a better school system for your kids, these are all potential actions that offer added personal incentives. It's my favorite money philosophy because it empowers us to believe that we can reach our greatest potential and that we can actually take control of what it means to be "rich."

This, of course, is not to dismiss the value of investing in real estate, the stock market, or your 401k. Those incredible moneymaking vehicles definitely deserve our attention. But when all is said and done, you can expect much better returns when you invest in yourself. How do you decide whether such an investment is worthwhile? These three steps will help:

1. **Recap what it means to be and feel fulfilled and satisfied in your life.** What kind of financial and emotional stability are you looking for, and how will this personal investment, whether it's going back to school, starting a new relationship, or launching a business, be a complement?

2. **Revisit your goals.** Understand how this personal endeavor can support your short- and long-term goals. Also make sure you understand if and how this personal investment may compromise any of your goals.

3. **Figure out how to make the most of the investment.** This is the best part about investing in yourself: You can control the outcome far more than the outcome of, say, investing in stocks or real estate. If you can visualize how to take the knowledge and experience of this investment and turn it into a positive difference in your life, it might be worth it.

Worthy Banking: Making the Most of Your Earnings

Making worthy financial decisions relates not only to how you spend, but also to how you save and invest. I got my first savings account with the help of my dad when I was a teenager. We opened it at the local credit union where my parents did their banking, and I don't even remember if we discussed interest rates. We probably did, but I don't think I quite understood the importance of earning a few pennies on the dollar. But the truth is, by making small adjustments, you can significantly improve savings. The following three adjustments will offer immediate results.

Adjustment 1: Land the Best Rate

You might think there's no difference between earning 1.5% or 1.75% on a savings account, but rest assured, a little bit can go a very long way. Suppose, for instance, you start the year off with $10,000 in an account earning 1.5%, and your friend begins with $10,000 in an account earning 1.75%. You each diligently add $5,000 a year to your accounts for the next five years. By 2015, your friend will be $2,000 richer, and all because he did some research and secured a better rate.

Adjustment 2: Ladder CDs

Are you familiar with certificates of deposit? Different CDs carry different maturities and interest rates. Typically, the longer the maturity date, the greater the interest rate. For example, a one-year CD may carry a 2.5% interest rate, a two-year CD a 3.0% interest rate, and a three-year CD a 3.50% interest rate. It may seem logical to want to put all your money in the three-year CD because it earns the highest rate. But actually there's a better strategy. By *laddering* your CDs, you spread out your savings into multiple CDs with various maturities and interest rates. Every time a CD expires, you redeposit that money into whichever CD has the longest maturity in your original CD ladder. In this case, it would be a new three-year CD, which may have an even higher rate of return at this point. By staggering out the savings, you can potentially maximize your rate of return and boost liquidity. By rolling from one CD to another, you also avoid the risk of locking into one single rate. If interest rates rise, you can still benefit from them. There are online calculators, such as at Bankrate.com, Bankingmyway.com, and CalculatorPlus.com, that can help you crunch the numbers.

Adjustment 3: Avoid Fees

Banks earn most of their revenue just from fees (billions of dollars a year, from overdraft fees, minimum balance requirement fees, ATM fees, transfer fees, and so forth). ATM fees alone are enough to eat up hundreds of dollars a year from your savings account. Do you even earn hundreds of dollars in interest in that account? Probably not, which means you are definitely getting a raw deal. To make your money work harder for you, sign up for fee-free checking accounts, link your checking and savings account together to lessen the risk of having insufficient funds, and learn the locations of your bank's fee-free ATMs between work and home to avoid paying usage fees at nonmember banks.

My Story:
When Having Debt Is Worth It

One of my readers wrote into my website at Farnoosh.TV desperate to understand why her husband opted not to pay down the mortgage ahead of schedule. He had explained it was because he could get a better return investing that money in the stock market. But for her, paying down the mortgage seemed like a more secure thing to do. Another perplexed reader asked me whether he should pay off his $5,000 car loan, which had a historically low 3.9% APR. He mentioned he was only earning .01% in his savings account.

What both readers fundamentally wanted to know is this: Are some debts good (worthy) debts? The answer is yes, some are, but that depends on the type of debt and the pros and cons of paying it off early. For instance, a con would be any penalties that might apply for paying off the debt early. Keep in mind that the pros and cons can be both financial and psychological. To make an informed decision, use the same analysis as when considering a big-ticket purchase. You must first determine affordability and then consider utility and risks.

Let's tackle both reader questions:

Should I Pay Off My Mortgage Early?

Let's throw out some numbers to give this question more context. The couple has a $200,000, 30-year mortgage *with a 5.5% fixed interest rate. Monthly payments, inter-est plus principal, total $1,135. At the end of 30 years, the couple will have paid a total of $408,000 to the bank.*

The couple has an excess cash flow of $1,000 a month for saving and investing. The norm is for the husband to take $500 of that and invest in the couple's retirement portfo-lio each month, which currently holds $75,000. The expectation is an average 8% return over the long run. The other $500 goes into a rainy-day fund that's already enough for eight-months of living expenses, or close to $40,000. The interest rate on that savings account is about 2%.

Pros to paying down the mortgage early: If the couple reroutes $500 toward the mortgage principal, they could save close to $115,000 in interest fees and own their home in half as many years, 15 instead of 30 years. The financial burden will be lifted in half the time, and the couple can sleep better at night knowing the roof over their heads is theirs and not the bank's. By putting money toward the mortgage, the couple also avoids pay-ing additional income tax on any interest earned in a savings account.

What are the cons? If the couple neglects to put $500 toward savings, they miss out on their rainy-day savings account reaching $158,000 in 15 years or $319,000 in 30 years, assuming an average 2% return rate over time. Would they prefer to stay liquid? As for the investment portfolio, if $500 was rerouted from that account to the mortgage, the couple misses out on a buildup of more than $413,000 in just 15 years at that 8% rate.

The Verdict

My advice is to keep investing $500 a month in their retirement portfolio. The interest there is unbeatable in the long run and best addresses the couple's retirement needs. Meantime, they should reroute the other $500 from savings to the mortgage principal. The couple already has a fat cushion for a rainy day; the possibility of being relieved of their mortgage in just 15 years is both financially and emotionally cathartic. And by the way, if the couple wants to continue saving in their rainy-day fund and put just one extra payment a year toward the principal, that would still go a long way. By doing this, they would save more than $40,000 in interest and be able to retire their mortgage five years sooner!

Should I Pay Down My Car Early?

My reader says he has only $5,000 left on his car loan with a 3.9% interest rate. He's been paying the loan down since 2006. Monthly payments total $290. He has 18 more payments left. I ask him about his liquidity. "$15,000," he says. "If I suddenly lost my job and needed an emergency fund, I think I'd be okay since I could use the remaining $10,000 and use my 0% interest credit card (a teaser rate for the first 12 months)." He also has *no credit card debt. Should he pay down his car loan early?*

Pros and cons: The pros are pretty clear. If he pays down the car loan, he immediately frees up an extra $290 a month that he could add to his liquid savings. He'd also save $220 in interest by paying the loan down immediately. In addition, his credit score—which is already at 780, he tells me—would benefit even further from reducing this outstanding debt. On the con side, the interest rate is so low on this car loan that he's only paying an extra $220 for stretching out the payments five more years. Is that better than taking a huge stash of money out of his savings account, which might leave him vulnerable in an emergency? True, he may be able to resort to a 0% APR credit card, but that's still a risk since he'd have to pay that back at some point and the interest rate will jack up after 12 months.

The Verdict

My advice to the reader is to pay down the car early. His finances are pretty stable, and getting this liability off his personal balance sheet is comforting. I advise him to continue to act like he still has a car payment, though, and pay himself to make up for the $5,000 hole in his rainy-day savings. And that .01% rate? He can do a whole lot better by moving his account to an online bank where savings rates are generally much higher.

"Worthy" in Action

Let's put this formula to the test with a couple of hypothetical cases. Because "worthy" choices have an element of subjectivity, I'm not going to conclude each case study with a definite "worthy" or "unworthy" stamp. The point is to walk through all the necessary analysis and consider both options—and even potential modifications.

Case Study 1

Charles and Mary are married, in their early 30s, and live in Northern California. Both are full-time faculty members at a university. Charles teaches political science. Mary teaches statistics. Their joint monthly take-home pay is roughly $8,000 a month, and their expenses average $6,500 a month. Net: $1,500 a month.

They've been hacking away at their credit card debt since getting married and have reduced it to approximately $5,000 from $15,000 in less than two years. Their goal is to be debt free in the next eight months, which means they need to allocate at least $650 a month toward that credit card debt, including interest and principal. They plan to use their excess cash flow of $1,500 to afford the fast payoff. Fortunately, they have no other debt besides their mortgage. Rainy-day savings equal $40,000. Retirement savings: $75,000. Job security? Both work in higher education, and although there's been some downsizing recently at their university, they have not been affected and don't expect to be.

Would buying a new SUV for $30,000 be worth it to them? Let's use our equation of comfortable affordability + good utility + manageable risks.

Comfortable Affordability?

What's their income security? No one can ever really be too certain about the safety of a job, but Charles and Mary believe they're not in as risky an industry as real estate or retail, which have seen greater rates of downsizing in their region recently. Mary has a little craft business on the Web and earns about $500 a month selling home-made jewelry on Etsy.com. She always thought if she lost her job, she'd try to make more out of that hobby and use the earnings to pay down their mortgage. It's not a certifiable backup plan, but the money does come in handy for impromptu expenses like baby shower gifts, restaurant dining, and the occasional parking ticket. In short, the couple's income security is above average.

Are they living below their means? Yes. They are netting $1,500 a month after their monthly expenses, with the goal of putting $650 of that toward credit card debt for the next eight months. The rest of their excess cash is used for discretionary things like vacations, clothes, and *maybe a new car.* We'll see....

Do they have enough savings? Yes. The couple has about six months of living expenses socked away in an online savings account earning a top rate (excellent!) and $75,000 in their combined retirement accounts, to which they add monthly from their pretax earnings.

How will they financially afford it? What's the plan? Charles plans on trading in his sedan (which he's had for seven years and finished paying off four years ago) for the new SUV. The blue book value of his car is about $7,000, so that should bring down the cost of the SUV to $23,000, plus another $3,000 for sales tax, title, and registration costs. They plan to finance the $26,000 total with a loan from their local credit union. With a 48-month, 6.4% auto loan, the couple's looking at $615 a month in car payments for the next four years. This expense will come out of their monthly net of $1,500.

With $1,500 disposable income each month, the money is certainly available to pay down the loan in four years and help pay down outstanding debt, one of the couple's priorities. If the numbers came up short, they would know to stop right here and start considering more affordable alternatives to the $30,000 SUV.

Good Utility?

What are the benefits of the new car? They love that it has twice the cargo room, which comes in handy since both are sporty and carry around golf clubs and tennis racquets in their current smaller trunks. The couple also goes on ski trips in the winter, and it would be nice to fit all their gear in the car—not to mention plow through the snow. And if they ever get a pet (or have a baby), the extra space in the car will certainly help out then, as well. They also decide that money spent would outweigh the benefits of any other purchases in this price range.

Manageable Risks?

Financial downsides? Financially the car isn't going to help them save any money—especially when you factor in the added gas and maintenance. But the couple feels confident this won't stretch their budget much. And if it does, they'll drive it less and carpool in Mary's hybrid car.

How does this expense potentially interfere with future planned expenses, and how do they plan to offset the interference? They think this one through and confess wanting to start a family in the next two years. They understand the expenses related to having a newborn can be at least $10,000 in the first year. They also want to renovate their kitchen in the next five years, and estimate that at $30,000. They also want to continue saving and, once again, be debt free from credit cards before anything else. Buying a new car now and paying an estimated $615 a month may slow down their current savings rate, but the couple believes they can allocate their entire year-end bonuses over the next few years toward saving for the baby and the renovations. Typically, they'd use all their year-end bonus money on vacations, but understanding that the new car will eat up some disposable income, they're committed to saving their bonus money (usually $10,000 total) for these short-term savings goals.

The Final Verdict for Charles and Mary

For this couple, buying a $30,000 car won't affect their finances too much. It's arguably *affordable*, but whether it's *worth it* is really a question of whether or not they'd like to use that extra money at the end of the month toward something else. We know their goals over the next few years include starting a family and renovating the kitchen. Would they rather save that $615 a month and speed up their kitchen renovation project? Maybe have two kids rather than one in the next few years? Skipping the car will also mean having more freedom to spend and use their year-end bonuses on vacations. Charles's car is only seven years old and has fewer than 100,000 miles on it. Surely, it can run smoothly for another few years. Do they really need the new car?

At this point, there's no right or wrong answer. Whether the couple decides yes or no, they'll have made a more conscious and educated decision…and that's a really good thing.

Keep in mind that sometimes the final answer doesn't have to be a flat out no. Sometimes financial moves aren't worth it *at the moment* but might be down the road. What about the couple waiting a year to buy the car? Or just waiting until they're free of debt in eight months, at which point they might qualify for a lower interest rate on the car and thus reduce their monthly payments? By then, too, one of them might be making more money to help make the payments. In the meantime, they could just use Mary's car so that Charles's car doesn't add more mileage or wear and tear. If they were to do that, they could still sell it for about $7,000 in a year's time. What's more, if they can even save an extra $500 a month in an interest-bearing account specifically for the new car, they'll have close to another $6,000, totaling about $13,000 for a down payment. Their monthly payments at that point (with even the same financing) would just be around $400, including sales tax and title and registration costs. The takeaway? *Sometimes waiting makes it all the more worthwhile. Call it delayed gratification.*

Case Study 2

Laura is a 29-year-old financial analyst from Boston, Massachusetts. After six years working for a large investment firm, she wants to quit the finance industry and go to nursing school to become an RN. She knows she won't necessarily make as much money in that line of work but is looking for more job security and has always been quietly fascinated by the medical field. Through some research, she's discovered she can go on an accelerated path toward achieving the degree. The Accelerated BSN (Bachelor of Science in Nursing) programs are available for those who already have a Bachelor degree or higher degree in another field and who are interested in moving into nursing quickly, like Laura, and typically last 12 to 18 months. Laura figures the faster she can get out of school, the faster she can start making money and paying off her student loans.

Will the leap to nursing school and the transition from one industry to another be worth it for Laura in the end? Let's dig.

Comfortable Affordability?

How much will the Accelerated BSN cost Laura? Tuition and fees alone average out to about $30,000. Does Laura have debt? At present, she has no credit card debt. Her salary has afforded her a comfortable life, and she has consistently tucked money away each month. She also has no student loans or a mortgage; she's currently renting her apartment.

What's her savings? Right now, she has $30,000 in liquid savings and another $30,000 in retirement savings.

Good Utility

What are the benefits? After seeing so many colleagues laid off over the past two years, Laura questions the long-term security of the financial services industry, an industry she's not even that passionate about. For her, a transition to nursing offers several psychological benefits. First, it offers peace of mind, knowing the industry is stable.

As boomers retire and the demand for healthcare soars, the number of nursing jobs is expected to increase through 2016, with an additional 587,000 new jobs (or 23% growth) over that period, according to the Department of Labor. That's higher than the national average of all other occupations, which are expected to show 7% to 13% growth. (She's clearly done her research.) Beyond that, becoming a nurse would make her happier, plain and simple. Her desk job at the financial firm is slowly but surely eating away at her happiness. Laura is someone who prefers to interact with and help others. Plus, she's always been curious about the medical world. And although her current job pays a generous salary, she's not attached to the lifestyle it affords.

Manageable Risks?

Would Laura be willing to move cities? There are no accelerated nursing programs in the Boston area, and this may be a red flag. To manage this risk, Laura must accept that if she wants to find work right away, she might need to be flexible and willing to move, especially to far-off regions in Arizona, Texas, and the Midwest, where nursing staff are in relatively short supply. Northeast hospitals, meanwhile, have plenty of applicants and few spots to offer to new graduates. Of course, once her career gets going, jobs will be open, regardless of the locale. Laura doesn't have a family or other dependents at this point, and so she decides she is willing to move to where the best job openings are.

Can she adjust to a lower salary? At present, Laura earns $120,000 a year plus a bonus of roughly $20,000 annually. In the nursing world, the pay is solid, but not as lucrative—at least not immediately. RNs earned, on average, a little more than $56,000 in 2007. The highest 10% brought home an average annual income of $83,000.

Can she handle the stress? Many nurses will tell you their jobs are not easy. Some may even compare the stress level to that of working at a trading desk on Wall Street; instead of people's money, however, you're responsible for people's lives. Although Laura might find this career more interesting, she won't exactly be leaving the pressure of her finance job behind.

The Final Verdict for Laura

Laura has many potential risk factors to weigh and consider here. She wonders whether she's underestimating how well she can manage after school with student loans, a lower-paying job, the stress of nursing, and possibly moving to another state. Did the recession just scare her to the point of wanting to ditch her current industry? Switching careers would be a huge game changer for Laura. While she can ultimately "afford" the cost of tuition, she wonders if she'll miss her current life too much? The goal here is not to scare Laura into staying put (discussed as "paralysis" in previous chapters). The goal of this exercise, as it was with Charles and Mary, is to fully examine the potential realities of a financial decision, both positive and negative. Laura's decision will ultimately depend on her personality, her tolerance for risk, and her commitment to achieving this goal. Perhaps what she needs is more time to think, more time to talk to her current boss to consider other responsibilities she might pursue if her current track is unfulfilling. Feeling insecure about a job or an industry is common, especially during a recession. During the recession of the late 2000s, the unemployment rate soared to 10%. In the midst of it all, I'll never forget former President Bill Clinton's appearance on one of the Sunday morning political programs. On that program, he recommended out-of-work Americans, especially recent grads, to consider investing in themselves by going back to school. As Clinton explained, it would be a great way to acquire new skills and boost their hiring and salary potential, and might even lead them to switch industries. For Laura, she might want to speak with more nurses, especially those who have transitioned from different careers so that she can understand what they see as pros and cons and get a sense of how they all cope. In the end, she'll come to a clear choice with few regrets, if any, and all because she took the time to aim for a *worthy* decision.

For all others considering grad school, remember that it isn't for everyone: It might cost too much money, it might be unnecessary in your field, or maybe you just don't feel like studying (or all of the above). It's no secret, after all, that continuing your education costs a lot of dough, unless you score a scholarship or your employer pays. According to the College Board, graduate students on average assume close to $13,000 a year in federal loans, and it's not uncommon for law and business school students to pile on more than $100,000 in debt.

So, how can you determine whether a financial move is worth it? If it complements your goals and you can find a way to make it work—financially and practically—it's probably worth every bit of your time and dime.

[1] Phone interview with Dan Ariely.

[2] Antonio Rangel, "Marketing Actions Can Modulate Neural Representations of Experienced Pleasantness," *Proceedings of the National Academy of Sciences*, January 2008.

[3] "Should You Buy This Now?" *Consumer Reports*, January 15, 2010.

[4] Electronic Retailing Association

[5] Dan Ariely, *Predictably Irrational* (HarperCollins, 2008), p. 20.

8

Think Five Years Ahead

"A good plan today is better than a perfect plan tomorrow."
General George S. Patton

When it comes to our life savings, we often refer to two primary buckets: rainy day and retirement. We save for short-term emergencies such as a layoff, car accident, or sudden medical procedure. For retirement, we have 401ks, IRAs, and other investment portfolios to help aggressively build savings for the future. At best, we live in the now, plan for the uncertainties, and invest for life 20, 30, or 40 years down the road. But what about everything else in between? What about all those tremendous milestones that help shape the purpose and meaning of life? Events such as starting a family, buying a home, changing careers, getting married (and divorced), and a sudden loss in the family? For those events, we tend to just fly by the seat of our pants and hope we'll have the means and resources to handle them when they occur. It's true that people prepare for some events—like a wedding or a baby—a year in advance, but they often still feel a bit uncomfortable when the time arrives.

Dealing with life's personal finances shouldn't have to feel like a 911 emergency, but extreme situations are not uncommon. Managing your finances in emergency situations—paying down debt after a sudden job loss, dealing with student loans, getting back on track after a pricey divorce—is not ideal. You need a plan that is ready to go if and when something bad happens to your finances. Neglecting to prepare as best we can for both the potential positive and *negative* outcomes of a given situation can prove unnecessarily stressful and burdensome, emotionally and financially.

To that end, we need a good in-between measure, a point of view that can help us better plan and prepare for our goals and when life *happens,* a thought strategy that's not as immediate as six-months down the road and not as intangible or distant as retirement.

The answer: *a five-year lens.* By now, we should know ourselves well enough to predict what we may need and want personally and professionally over the next five years. And if we're not 100% sure, we can at least make some pretty good guesses. For example, at the moment, I'm 30 years old and unmarried. I know I want to tie the knot and start a family in the next five years, and so far I'm on a hopeful track. My boyfriend and I have been together for almost four years. We've discussed marriage and agree we're going to make the leap soon (and yes, as a couple, not separately). If all goes as expected, our future, including marriage, children, and a Labrador Retriever, will no doubt be a complete life and financial game changer. So with that in mind, what can I do now to ensure these events won't startle my bank account and my savings? What risks can I expect in the meantime as I strive to hit my five-year marks?

You think this is unnecessary premeditation? You like to live life a bit more spontaneously, you say? Well, here's the thing. A proper five-year compass is not designed to be a buzz kill. It's simply a useful strategy to prepare you for the expected and unexpected. A five-year strategy lets you manage your money and your goals at a more consistent and tangible pace. Even if you don't hit all your goals in the next five years, the discipline and focus you gain from sticking to a five-year plan will ensure your money stays safe and well managed.

Know Where You Stand

The money meetings on *Bank of Mom & Dad* begin by covering the first step in conquering your goals: to get real and accept responsibility for your financial life. Own up to it and don't be afraid to learn that you *haven't* yet been doing the best job.

To start, evaluate your current financial picture by answering the following questions:

- How much savings do I have right now? Know every penny.
- How much debt do I have right now? Again, know every penny.
- What's my credit score? (Clue: 740 and above is terrific; anything lower and you may want to work at boosting your score by consistently paying bills on time and paying down debt.)
- What is my job security at this moment? Be honest and consider your industry and your performance.
- What are my problem areas when it comes to managing my money and why? Do I often pay bills late? Do I have recurring debt? What are my money drains and what am I doing (if anything) to combat them? If I'm sinking in debt, am I seeking professional help? Have I made more payments toward debt? Do I see a light at the end of the tunnel?

Know Where You Want to Go

From there, list your five-year personal, financial, and professional goals as specifically as you can. This is similar to the practice from the second chapter, but this time you want to think about explicit milestones you want to cross five years out. What would you like to see change for the better? Do you want to make more money? How much more? Do you want to switch careers? If so, what do you want to transition toward? Will you want to help support an older family member, like a parent or grandparent? How much time and money might that cost? Do you hope to get married? Have children? Move to a new part of town? A bigger house? Granted, again, you might not be able to draw out a descriptive five-year map of goals. You may not know whether you absolutely want to raise a family in the next few years or if you will stay at your current job, but being conscious of and prepared for the *possibilities* can still help as you manage your money and your five-year compass.

Be Pessimistic *Enough*

As you imagine your life in the next five years, it's important to consider all the possibilities, the good and the bad. I'm going to disagree with my mother here for a moment (the eternal optimist) and say that sometimes in life you have to acknowledge potential hardships and risks that may come your way. Pessimism, in some ways, can pay off. Barbara Ehrenreich, the best-selling author of *Nickel and Dimed*, recently published a new book titled *Bright-Sided*, which criticizes the highly marketed ideology and industry of "positive thinking." She posits that all the smiley-faced hype has kept individuals from considering negative outcomes and, in turn, they become victims of their own overzealousness. It's a valid point, and she provides strong examples to support her theory (ahem, our recent housing and stock market crash).

For your financial house to be completely in order, it's critical to be somewhat, even slightly, pessimistic. I don't want you to let pessimism cloud your journey or keep you from exploring new opportunities. The hope is that a little pessimism can serve as a shield against some of life's real risks because it ensures preparedness.

In a 2002 interview with *Forbes* magazine, Nobel laureate Daniel Khaneman, around the time he was awarded his prize for his work on irrationality, discussed his thinking about optimism, saying that it was a wonderful thing. "There are contexts where optimism helps. Generally where it helps is in executing plans. It keeps you on track. It gives you energy to overcome obstacles…It keeps you healthy and it keeps you resilient." But personally, he said, he would not want his financial advisor to be optimistic. "I'd like him to be as realistic as possible."[1]

His reasoning was that there's no harm in understanding the odds of a particular decision. In our own lives, too much optimism can sometimes lead to overconfidence and a false sense of security when taking on real risks.

Now, about those risks: The two primary types are the sort you control and the sort you can't. The risks we can control are those we bring upon ourselves...when we sign on to an adjustable rate mortgage, neglect to stick to a budget, or fail to pay down debt aggressively. In the example scenarios, we risk staying in a cycle of debt and damaging our credit. The biggest, perhaps, is failing to save on a consistent basis and not having enough money in an emergency or to fulfill our goals. Separately, some risks are *beyond* our control, such as a stock market crash, an unexpected illness that forces you to pay out of pocket, or a job loss.

What follows is an approach that will help protect you from both types of risks.

Develop Your Strategy

Your financial strategy is a plan of attack against risk and unforeseen events, plotted against goals, wants, and needs (for today through to a specified time in the future). With your financial reality firmly grasped, you can begin to lay the foundation of a viable financial future. Be sure to set up detours and preemptive strikes to deal with potential risks from a job loss to a recession to your own overspending. Know how you will pay down debt and save, and how you'll measure and keep tabs on your progress.

Indiscriminating Five-Year Risk: The Next Recession

Before we get too deep into our five-year plans, let's recognize some highly probably risks we will face (sometimes more than once): The first is a recession, or at the least a "market correction." The need for a five-year plan was reinforced during the recent downturn in our

economy, a downturn that, looking back, we really should have antic-
ipated. But instead, when the stock market crashed and unemployment soared, panic and a contagion of fear broke out. Uncertain as to
how to react, many Americans made some poor choices. They pulled
out of the stock market, quit investing in their 401k plans, and lost
confidence in all that they'd built up over the previous five years.
Their emotions got the better of them and to the better of their
money.

My Story: When Does Cashing Out Make Sense?

*One of the best pieces of advice I heard occurred on
Monday, October 6, 2008, on the* Today Show. *It came
from Jim Cramer, who told America that if they had any
money in the stock market that they absolutely needed in
the next five years, whether to help send their kids to college or retire, they should to turn it to cash. For those
who could afford to withstand the turmoil in the market
(for example, parents with 529 college savings plans that
still had ten years until maturity), Cramer said to go
ahead and "ride it out."*

*The media was up in arms over Cramer's directions. So,
during our daily show,* Wall Street Confidential *on
TheStreet.com TV, I asked Jim for some clarification,
because much of the mainstream media was interpreting
his statement as a call for all people to flee the stock market. But, of course, that's not what he meant. Jim
explained, if you lost your job tomorrow and saw your
stock portfolio plummet in the next few weeks, would you*

still be able to get by and hit your five-year goals with your investments? Rising unemployment and stock market losses were risks Americans were likely facing, and so Cramer's advice was to think ahead by five years. If you were dependent on the profits from your stock market investments between now and the next five years for any major goals such as college tuition or a down payment on a home, he suggested taking a less-risky approach and shifting those investments to safer havens like cash or bonds.

Cramer was right to be cautious. The days that followed would mark the worst week in stock market history. Between Monday, October 6 and Friday, October 10, 2008, the Dow Jones Industrial Average plunged 1,874 points, losing nearly 20% of its value. It took more than a year for the Dow—and the overall stock market—to bounce back, but the market is still an unpredictable beast. I'm not sure anyone who followed Cramer's advice really regrets holding on to their cash as they watched the market deteriorate in the days, weeks, and months that followed. Maybe they needed that money to send a child to college in the upcoming year. Maybe they needed the money for a down payment on a new home in a couple of years. How might their five-year goals have changed if all that money was tied up in the stock market?

As history has proven, our economy is not done with recessions. We've averaged a downturn about every five or so years since the Panic of 1797. According to the National Bureau of Economic Research, a trusted resource on recessions among economists, policy makers, and academia, a recession is defined as "a significant decline in economic activity spread across the country, lasting more than a few months."[2] Always count on a recession in your five-year plan. Don't take too much risk with your investments, especially if they're meant to cover short-term goals. There are several ways to play the cash card (e.g., U.S. Treasury bills, certificates of deposit, money market mutual funds). Investors embraced this approach over the past two years, distinctly transitioning away from equities and over to the cash market. In June 2008, researchers at Merrill Lynch found investors moved away from the stock market at a record rate. Twenty seven percent of fund managers were "underweight" stocks, the most in ten years. The same month, 42% of money managers were "overweight" cash, up from 31% in May.[3]

Todd Harrison, the founder of Minyanville.com, told me that in times of great financial difficulty, the winning formula includes discipline, not so much conviction. In other words, stay rational. Don't take risks that might jeopardize your near-term goals. The best strategy during volatile financial times is to stay calm and focused.

When markets are too good to be true, know that those happy days are likely to end soon and won't return for some time. Although it's almost impossible to precisely anticipate these downturns, the five-year lens should be helpful enough when mapping out your financial strategy. Just because the economy decides to take a breather doesn't mean your goals have to.

Indiscriminating Five-Year Risk: A Job Loss

At the height of the recent unemployment crisis in our country, you had about a one in ten chance of finding yourself out of work, and probably higher if your job was in real estate, finance, or in a mall.

And the scariest thing about layoffs is that you're often completely blindsided. In fact, a 2009 survey by Harris Interactive found that employees usually think the guy or gal in the nearby cubicle is more likely to get the axe than them. During one of my college internships, a manager told me that a sure sign of layoffs approaching is when the top boss alerts the entire staff to an impromptu "mandatory meeting" in a conference room.

I don't need to explain how getting laid off can be a deeply emotional experience, but I do need to remind you to not let your feelings get in the way of protecting your finances. A layoff or sudden firing is a fact of life, and regaining your financial footing can take several months. In 2009, the average job hunt lasted six to seven months. That is why I and other financial experts emphasize the importance of having at least a six-month rainy-day savings cushion.

Your five-year strategy should include doing all that you can to secure employment and prepare for an unfortunate turn of events. Having the savings cushion is integral. In addition, here are some other protective measures you should be prepared to take quickly in case of a layoff:

> **Know your rights.** If your employer offers you a severance package, remember that you can negotiate before signing. Keep in mind, too, that you are legally allowed to receive any and all accrued vacation time. Keep your employee guidebook handy to refer to your employee rights. As for any vested stock options you own, you typically have 3 months or 90 days after the date you got laid off to exercise those options. Some companies may even extend that period. If you are a contract employee, go through your paperwork to understand your rights. Perhaps you had a three-year contract and you only worked at the company for one year. The contract may have a clause that protects you from early termination, and you may be able to earn compensation for the remaining time on your

contract. Hiring a labor attorney for a couple hours of her time to review your severance package and your contract may be money well spent, especially if you feel you're getting a raw deal.

Apply for unemployment benefits ASAP. During times of high unemployment, when many more individuals are applying for unemployment insurance from the state, there may be a wait of several weeks from when you apply to when you actually start receiving your benefits. The good news is that once you start collecting unemployment, the payout is retroactive from the date you applied. In most states, you can apply over the phone or online. Visit the Department of Labor's website at www.dol.gov for details on eligibility requirements, as well as where to apply for benefits.

Secure health insurance. Again, do this as soon as possible. You need to notify your healthcare provider that you want to enroll in COBRA within 30 days of getting laid off. If your former employer was sponsoring your health insurance plan and continues to sponsor health insurance for its existing employees, you can apply for COBRA, which provides up to 18 months of health insurance to those who've been laid off or left their jobs voluntarily and under good terms. If you got fired under bad terms or laid off because your company went bankrupt, you more than likely won't be eligible for COBRA. Your company's human resources department should have the application information or you can go to www.dol.gov. A note of caution: COBRA can be pricey because you have to pay the entire cost your employer pays plus a 2% administrative fee. Monthly COBRA premiums can easily run up to $400 for single coverage and $1,200 for family coverage. For some more affordable alternatives, check with your spouse or partner. If your wife, husband, or partner is getting insurance from his or her employer, see whether you can piggyback. If you don't fall into that category but you're still young and healthy, consider an individual policy by shopping online and comparing rates at sites like eHealthInsurance.com and Esurance.com. Beyond that, there are ways to get health insurance with group discounts through union membership or by going through a professional organization. Still others have been known to take courses part time at a local school, where you may be able to get group health insurance. If you have kids, contact your state's children's health insurance program to see whether they are eligible for coverage at www.chipmedicaid.org.

Protect your 401k. You might be tempted to cash it out, but remember that your 401k is for the golden years and not to pay for living expenses now. Significant tax penalties apply to an early withdrawal from your 401k before age 59 1/2. The best thing to do is to either leave your money in the existing account until you get another job and roll the money into your new employer's 401k plan or roll that money penalty free through a direct transfer into an individual retirement account or IRA.

Milestone Math

What can happen during the five-year allotment runs the gamut from weddings to first-borns, buying a new home, starting a business, and going back to school. Here's what these milestones roughly cost—on average—and what you need to know ahead of time.

Wedding and Marriage

The average cost of a wedding in the United States is between $21,000 and $24,000, according to the Association for Wedding Professionals International. That's not including the rings or the honeymoon. Meantime, in fancy ZIP codes like Manhattan and San Francisco, wedding costs can easily be more than double the national average. The earlier you start planning, the earlier you can commit to saving for the big day and your new life together. My advice to engaged couples is to consider living on one partner's salary for a few months up to the wedding to not only help pay for the bash but also to start building a joint nest egg. And just as important as saving, you want to pay off those towering credit card balances, too. If you have bad credit or high levels of debt, commit to improving your financial mess before marriage. In 2009, I heard from a distraught reader who—only after marrying her beau—discovered his credit score was in the 500s (out of 850). Ouch. Now as the couple plans to buy their first home, they're hitting roadblocks. If they file jointly for a mortgage, banks will likely reject them based on his poor credit or slap them with an exorbitant interest rate. But if she files alone for a mortgage, they won't be able to qualify for as big of a loan because the bank will consider only her income. Their plans to buy a home are now on the back burner as the couple plays catch up in the credit arena. Had this been discussed before marriage, the couple could have invested their time and money more wisely to avoid this hurdle.

Your First House

At last check, the median price of a single-family home in the United States was roughly $178,000, according to data from the National Association of Realtors. Since the credit crisis, banks have not been as open-armed with loans, in particular with mortgages. That means borrowers need to be extra squeaky-clean and secure when applying for credit. You want to show that you have cash in the bank, a secure income, and a clean bill of credit. Before the recession, a 0% down payment was not unheard of. Today, expect to have 15% to 20% in cash to put down, with an additional cash reserve in your savings account totaling the first year's property taxes. If you work for yourself, banks like to see two years of steady income (likewise, if you are employed by a company). As for your credit, the best mortgage rates go to borrowers with credit scores in the 700s. Depending on your savings and your credit status, you may need to begin getting your act together a year or two in advance of applying for a mortgage. Six months before beginning your home search, get preapproved for a mortgage to know how much banks will lend you. Keep in mind that 99% of the time—even still in this post-recession era—you'll prequalify for more than you'll be comfortable spending. A safe rule of thumb: Avoid borrowing more than two-and-a-half times your annual income.

New Set of Wheels

Want to finance a $40,000 Beemer on a $55,000 salary? Think again.

Monthly payments for a new car plus its insurance and gas shouldn't exceed 15% to 20% of one's take-home pay. As with mortgages, banks prefer to give the best loan rates to borrowers with credit scores at least in the 700s. A 1% or 2% difference in your interest rate can save you thousands of dollars in interest payments over the life of the loan. A reliable car, safe neighborhood, and sound driving record can also lower the insurance rate. Another tip: Don't assume you have to finance the car through the auto dealership. Consumers can opt to use a less-expensive, third-party lender such as a local bank or credit union.

Baby

In year one, babies, on average cost $7,700, according to researchers at BabyCenter.com, a site for new and expecting parents. That doesn't include childcare, which can easily run an extra $1,000 a month. With the use of BabyCenter.com's handy online calculator, I discovered that if I were to have a baby tomorrow, I'd need about $39,000, including the cost of childcare, to take care of my newborn for the first 12 months. Yeesh. The first financial must before parenthood: Wipe out any and all credit card debt. Try to start parenthood with a clean slate, since you're likely to incur a heap of additional costs preparing for and raising a child. Not to mention, if you need to take on any loans over the next few years (perhaps for a bigger home or a bigger car), banks prefer borrowers with a small credit-utilization ratio. That ratio is equal to your level of outstanding debt over your total available credit. Keep that ratio to less than 30% and pay all your bills on time to really polish your credit score. Next, don't worry about moving right away to a bigger space. Perhaps the biggest misconception about having a baby is that expectant parents need more room to provide for the child. False. Save your time, energy, and money while pregnant. The experts at BabyCenter.com tell me that an infant can probably sleep in a bassinet in the parents' room for the first six months, especially if being breastfed. If money's tight, don't worry about splurging on a fancy nursery, either. Instead, start a savings nest egg for all the day-to-day food and diaper costs in the first year. As soon as you learn that you're pregnant, consider putting aside as much as you can afford every week or month to help at least make it through your maternity leave. Another important preemptive strike against child costs is to know your healthcare rights, to fully understand the terms and conditions of your health insurance policy. Know whether your health care provider covers pre-natal to post-partum. In addition, at least six months before your scheduled delivery, sit down with your human resources manager to clarify how much you will be paid during your maternity leave (if at all). In some states, new moms can qualify for short-term disability, but that's also very limited pay. Finally, a great way to avoid many unnecessary costs related to pregnancy is to take care of you. Eating a healthful diet, taking vitamins, cutting back on caffeine, exercising throughout your pregnancy, and having a preconception checkup can all help reduce health risks.

Grad School

Priya Dasgupgta, GRE program manager at Kaplan Test Prep and Admissions, told me over 70% of students preparing for the GRE said they were "very" or "somewhat" concerned about taking on debt from grad school tuition and its related costs. That's based on a 2007 survey by Kaplan. It figures, since, on average, grad students owe about $30,000 upon completing a Master's program—also according to Kaplan. Begin by exhausting all financial resources. A year before the start of enrollment, fill out the FAFSA (Free Application for Federal Student Aid) at fafsa.ed.gov, which is the gateway to a large chunk of financial aid awarded to students.

Even though banks are getting out of the business of offering private student loans, that's no excuse to quit your search for funding. Talk to your local community bank or credit union that hasn't suffered from severe write-downs for available loan programs. Ask the student aid office in your graduate school for applications for private scholarships, school fellowships, and teaching assistantships. Also consider peer-to-peer lending websites, such as Prosper.com and Lending.com, which eliminate banks as middlemen and directly connect individual borrowers and lenders. Another savings strategy is to structure your schedule to work and go to school part time. It may be more time consuming and challenging, but it also eases the blow of graduate school tuition. Some employers may even contribute tuition expenses, if you agree to return to the same company full time upon graduation for a minimum number of years. The federal government actually encourages this with a special tax code letting employers pay as much as $5,250 a year in tuition for courses pertaining to your profession. Check with your human resources manager to learn about your company's education benefits program, often called the employer assistance program.

In the final two chapters of this book, we look at some alternative paths you might take to enhance your personal and financial satisfaction—and it all starts with getting out of your comfort zone.

[1] Forbes, "Nobel Laureate Debunks Economic Theory," November, 6, 2002.

[2] National Bureau of Economic Research, "Determination of the December 2007 Peak in Activity," December 11, 2008.

[3] Merrill Lynch Fund Manager Survey, June 18, 2008.

Part III

Raise the Bar

9

Break from the Norm

"Do one thing every day that scares you."

Eleanor Roosevelt

As my mom often says to my brother and me when we are too hesitant to try something new, "You'll never know your true potential unless you get out of your comfort zone." My mom and the brainy folks at Google think alike. Engineers at the search engine giant dedicate 20% of their time, or one day per week, pursuing projects that take them down a whole new path, extracurricular assignments that pique their interests, separate from their normal responsibilities at work. Google calls its philosophy "Innovative Time Off" or "20% Time" and boasts the initiative has led to major corporate product launches from Gmail to AdSense. In all, the company estimates about half of its new products launched in the last six months of 2005 stemmed from this emphasis to be "creative" at work.[1]

At the core of Google's 20% rule is the theory that you can potentially boost your bottom line by exploring new thoughts and strategies. How might our personal lives improve if we actively dedicate a fraction of our time and resources to creative interests or alternative projects?

*What if we were to adopt a way of thinking that encourages us to
explore unconventional paths? It doesn't have to be grandiose. It can
be something small, a minor tweak or a slight derailment that can
help create even more financial momentum. Some risk may apply,
but the long-term benefits might end up outweighing the costs.*

Pursue something new. For example, pick up a few shares of
dicey stock, invest in a small business, start your own business (more
about that in Chapter 10, "Embrace the Entrepreneurial Spirit"), or
even write a book. Such endeavors are personally satisfying and have
the potential of building financial momentum. But what are the
obstacles?

Overcoming Risk Aversion

Breaking from the norm requires that you assume some risk. There
may be opportunity costs or financial risks. So, how does one get over
the fear of risk? It's not simple, say the experts, because people are
hardwired to avoid risk. Curtis Faith, a successful entrepreneur and
trader for the past 20 years and best-selling author of *Way of the
Turtle* and *Trading from Your Gut,* explained to me that society
encourages us toward safe decision making and following the rules.
"As a society, we beat risk taking out of people," Curtis told me.
"Look at our school system. If you're a nonconformist, the system is
against you from the beginning. You risk detention and teachers hat-
ing you. Teachers like kids who don't cause a fuss. And when you get
out to a world beyond school, most people continue being pushed
slowly toward this risk-averse idea that if you follow this prescribed
'path' that we set out for you, then your life will turn out wonderful.
In reality, that's not the case." He explained that this is a 70-year-old
mentality that goes back to the time our country's school system
became officially formalized. But as society evolves, more uncertainty
is naturally unleashed, and maintaining a risk-averse attitude can
actually be a dangerous thing. What you once considered to be risk

free is in fact no longer the case, whether it be investing in blue-chip stocks or taking a corporate job at a well-established firm. The key takeaway is that we must accept that there's no such thing as risk free, especially as our society and the economy changes. Pay attention to the potential for risk in all decisions, but don't miss important opportunities because you fear the risks.

Strategies for mastering risk that Curtis recommends include the following:

1. Embrace the fact that risk, in various forms, is everywhere.
2. Be prepared (financially and psychologically) to minimize risk by staying on top of things. Have a Plan B and be prepared to go to it if circumstances warrant.

Investing is still a sore spot for many Americans as we climb out of the recession, and understandably so. Many of our 401k portfolios got sliced in half, earning a new name: the 201k. If you ask Curtis, he'll tell you that the strategy of buy and hold, where you put x amount of money in stocks, bonds, and funds and ride out the market until retirement, is no longer the best way to manage risk (for obvious reasons). Instead, investors need to be willing to shift their allocations periodically to address the risks in the marketplace, while addressing their own personal needs.

If you want to beat the curve, review your investments once a month. If you are heavily invested in stocks and see that the S&P 500 keeps bouncing around a high level (say, 1,500, as it did in late 2008 before the market crashed), and you know you will need the cash currently tied up in shares for something critical sometime in the next five years, you should manage risk by adjusting away from high-risk investments to lower-risk instruments such as cash and bonds. When you're examining your portfolio each month, "Pay attention to long-term cycles, too," Curtis advises. That might be a lot to ask of us, since we tend to analyze short-term patterns, as some behavioral economists have concluded.

But, as Curtis reminded me, if you pay attention to historical trends, you should never really be caught by surprise. "It was apparent to anyone who was paying attention to the real estate market that the rise was unsustainable," says Curtis. "What's more," he says, "Lots of people were talking about it." So read the news and talk to older investors you know who can give their perspective on trends.

Finally, to manage risk, you have to be willing to lose (at least a little). "Any time you make a financial decision around uncertainty (i.e., risk), you have to be willing to be wrong," says Curtis. For example, you might see the trend reports on real estate and deduce that the gains cannot be sustained for much longer. You sell your condo, and for the next year or two, prices continue to go up. You feel like an utter loser. You have seller's remorse. That's a risk you might need to take, but in the long run it should pay off. In other words, be okay to leave the party early. "When you deal with uncertain outcomes, the right decision doesn't always result the way you expected it to. You have to play for the long run," says Curtis.

Timing Is Everything

Warren Buffet famously said that a key to investing well is to "be greedy when others are fearful."[2] And he's right. Opportunities present themselves when people are running for the hills. This signals a great time to consider alternative paths. Don't fear being contrary.

"A lot of major successful companies started during times of great stress, recession, and depression," says Victoria Colligan, founder of Ladies Who Launch. I interviewed Victoria in 2009 regarding the rising trend in female entrepreneurship during the recession. She wasn't surprised at all by the movement and referenced the Great Depression as an example of how individuals can embark on once-in-a-lifetime opportunities in down periods. Victoria reminded me that several blue chip companies got their start during the Great Depression, from Hewlett-Packard to McDonald's and United Technologies.

For some, breaking from the norm in hard times has partly to do with the "what do I have to lose" mentality, a mentality that can actually encourage people to take a chance. For others, a recession or depression presents fewer barriers to entry (e.g., bigger talent pool willing to work for less pay because of layoffs, cheaper real estate and technology, and more flexible ways of transacting business, such as bartering).

When 30-something moms Emily Meyer and Leigh Rawdon cofounded their children's clothing line, Tea Collection, it was right after the dot-com bust in the heart of Silicon Valley. "People said it was a crazy time to start," says Rawdon. "But looking back, timing was everything…A recession makes you incredibly disciplined about how you spend your money," she told me. "We thought 'if you can start a business now, imagine how stronger we'll be when the economy comes back.'" Today their clothing line is available worldwide.

Aside from starting a business, consumers snatched up deals during the recession—from homes at heavily discounted prices to beaten-down stocks that should one day afford them a more secure retirement. In fact, if you bought any of the depressed financial stocks at the depth of the recession, you probably made a nice profit less than a year later. Second-home market experts say a market slowdown and low interest rates create buying opportunities.

All said, breaking from the norm may require that you jump through a few extra hoops. While prices are down during a recession, banks might not be as willing to lend because of tight credit markets and the fear of defaulting borrowers. Banks are normally tough on second-home borrowers no matter the market conditions, but in a recession the standards are even higher. They assume if the borrower runs into financial hardship, the second home is likely the first property they'll default on. When preparing to buy a second home, ensure that you have maintained a particularly strong credit history, that you have a credit score well into the 700s, and can put down at least a 20% of the cost of the property as an initial payment.

Other options to consider when banks stop lending are to turn to peer-to-peer (P2P) lending websites or the "bank of friends and family." Research firm Celent reported that the overall P2P market will climb to $5.8 billion in loans in 2010, up 800% from 2009.[3] P2P is not only a creative way to borrow money and secure an interest rate that is probably lower than what financial institutions are offering, but it's also a way for lenders to earn more interest than leaving money in a savings account. Sure there are risks when lending to people, but the established sites like VirginMoney.com, Prosper.com, and Lending-Club.com are set up to encourage both parties to fulfill their contractual promises.

The recession also encouraged bartering, or the swapping of goods and services, as strapped individuals and business owners strove to spend less money in the new economy. I discussed this on the *Today Show* in 2009, picking up on a rise in new Internet sites catering to this rebirth of bartering. Sites such as Swaptree, U-Exchange, SwapGiant, and FavorPals were just a handful of new web businesses capitalizing on our renewed interest in bartering. Granted, bartering is not a "new" strategy, but to see a boom during hard times is evidence that people are creatively breaking from the norm. They're figuring out ways to get what they want without relying on the traditional methods (like paying cash or using a credit card), and both parties to the transaction get what they need.

To break from the norm is to simply get out of your comfort zone and open yourself up to a bigger world of opportunity in your personal, financial, and professional life. If we can commit to creativity, at least once a week as the Google folks do, we have a great chance of accomplishing our furthest goals in good times and especially in bad. Along the way, we also gain self-confidence and enhance our problem-solving skills.

Alternative Places for Your Investments

Investing in a Friend's Business

As we enter a new post-recession wave of entrepreneurship and as financial institutions continue to struggle with a tight credit market and restricted lending, you may be approached more and more to invest in a friend's or relative's business. When handing money to a friend or relative, you need to consider some key risks, including the impact on your relationship if things don't work out as planned. With good planning and execution, however, it's possible to mitigate risks, make a sound profit, and most important, keep your relationship intact.

The first step, before jumping into a business deal with someone close to you, is to understand the role you will play. Be clear about your motivations. Do you want an active role in the business and be involved in day-to-day decisions or do you want to be a silent partner? Do you care how your money gets invested? I interviewed an unhappy investor who complained that the $100,000 he gave to his friend for his start-up actually paid for the company car. He had hoped it would go toward hiring employees or establishing the storefront. Again, be clear about your expectations.

The next step is to do your due diligence. Go through your friend's business plan with a fine-tooth comb and read closely the sections on market size, competition, and the exit strategy. Call other friends and business contacts who have more knowledge of the type of business you're considering investing in. What are the barriers to entry, and why might your friend's business be in a good position to combat those hurdles? Review the financial strategy. If the numbers are too much to digest, call your finance friends or a small business counselor at Score.org for free advice.

Another topic to pursue is who will be in charge of the business. Your friend may have a brilliant business idea and plan, but he's not one to execute a bachelor party, let alone a full-on business.

Find out the number of investors involved in this business. Who else besides you is forking over money for the start-up? Ask whether he's gotten any bank loans. If he has, that may also be a positive indicator that this business plan has some legs. Even better is if your friend, himself, is putting in a significant portion of money, say 20% of the overall costs.

Finally, put everything in writing. Get legal help. The National Venture Capital Association, www.nvca.org, has free samples of legal documents, from term sheets to investor rights agreements.

Investing in Gold

Gold has become all the rage over the last decade, as more investors drool over this commodity's insane returns. By the start of 2010, the price of gold had rallied to more than $1,100 an ounce, compared to just $270 an ounce in 2001.

I wrote about gold for *Entrepreneur* and TheStreet.com—probably more than I would have liked—and learned there is a whole underground world of gold enthusiasts. So, what is it with all the *amour d'or?* For one, gold is considered to be a "safe-haven investment." It's viewed as a means to store value when all other financial instruments are depreciating (e.g., stocks, funds, the U.S. dollar). The price of gold tends to go up amid rising inflation, a weak U.S. dollar, and higher oil prices. What's more, gold insiders tell me, the precious metal has something going for it that other financial instruments don't in that it's not based on a government's or financial institution's promise; that is, it's not backed by debt. Instead, it's a tangible investment. You can hold it in your hands and it stays intact. The one great risk, of course, is that the price of gold is highly volatile. It can easily run up or down because of its small market supply.

Simon Constable, a former colleague of mine at TheStreet.com, is a bona-fide gold expert. Simon tells me that buying gold bullion coins is like buying financial insurance for your portfolio. It's basically acting as a hedge against catastrophic events occurring. If something bad happens, like a depression or financial catastrophe, gold should greatly appreciate in value. What if conditions suddenly improve, Simon? Is gold a complete bust at that point? "If nothing bad happens, then the gold will be a bad investment," he tells me. "But, hey, everything else will be superb," he quickly points out.

How does one go about buying gold? The Gold American Eagle Coin is the most widely traded gold bullion coin. The U.S government guarantees it by weight, content, and purity. There is a bit of a markup from the spot price of gold, mainly so the dealer can cover its costs. You can buy gold in more affordable ways. For example, you can purchase the Gold American Eagle coin in a fraction, as small as one-tenth. Retailers include Kitco.com, BlanchardGold.com, and UsaGold.com. There are also gold funds, which you can buy online through various brokerage sites.

As with all of these untraditional investments, you want to keep your exposure to gold limited, around 5% of a diversified portfolio, for the reasons we covered earlier. Also, this is a buy and hold investment. You want to keep gold for the long term, not to get rich quick. Gold experts don't usually recommend selling back your entire gold investments unless you really have to—somewhat like life insurance. It may be wiser to rebalance your exposure by selling a bit here and there when the market goes awry.

Investing in Private Equity

Michael Lazerow is a serial entrepreneur. The 34-year-old father of three has created at least four companies since his college days at Northwestern University, where he launched University Wire, a network of college newspapers, from his dorm room. He then sold the company to CBS, and soon after launched Golf.com, which would later be bought by Time Inc. Next, he started Lazerow Consulting and his newest venture, Buddy Media, an application development firm that works with social networking websites like Facebook.

If you're a risk taker like Lazerow, then investing in private equity might be your thing. It certainly has been a lucrative strategy for him. Briefly, investing in private equity means investing in companies that seize other companies and later sell them for a profit (at least that's the plan).

When I first dove into the inner workings of private equity, I suspected it was just a game for the rich to get richer. And it sure used to be. Traditionally, it was an exclusive society of high net-worth (i.e., more than $1 million in the bank) and in-the-know individuals like Lazerow and institutional investors, pension plans, and university endowments. Lazerow, himself, calls it a "clubby" investment.

But recently this members-only club opened its doors to invite the financial B-listers (i.e., the <$1 million in the bank crowd) to the party. Vista Research and Management has issued the Listed Private Equity Plus Fund (ticker: PRIVX), an open-end mutual fund that tracks private equity firms. You can begin investing with a minimum $1,000. To learn more, visit vrmfunds.com.

The PowerShares Global Listed Private Equity Portfolio (ticker: PSP) is another way to get in. The portfolio tracks the Red Rocks Listed Private Equity exchange-traded fund, which consists of 40 to 60 publicly traded companies tied to private equity.

With all these new ways to invest in private equity, it's still risky business. These should be considered long-term investments that you want to hold for an average five to ten years.

---

[1] Marissa Mayer, VP of Google Search Product and User Experience, Presentation at Stanford University, June 30, 2006.

[2] Warren Buffet, "Buy American, I Am." *New York Times*, October 16, 2008.

[3] Celent, "Top Tech Trends in Banking: 2008."

10

Embrace the Entrepreneurial Spirit

"Choose a job you love and you will never have to work a day in your life."

Confucius

Throughout the past decade while working in financial news, I've interviewed hundreds and hundreds of entrepreneurs, from domestic doyenne Martha Stewart to billionaire media maverick Mark Cuban to Ali and Hash Hafizi, the young, immigrant brothers who've run the "Good Morning America" coffee pushcart on Wall Street for almost 10 years. Their specialty buck-twenty-five brew is the morning must-have on Wall Street, with the brothers selling about 100 cups every hour—enough to help support their family of nine, including their mom, dad, and brothers and sisters, who all live under one roof just over the bridge in New Jersey. It's not confirmed, but I suspect the success of the Hafizi brothers' cart had something to do with the sudden closings of the competing Starbucks and Dunkin Donuts across the street.

At present, I am fascinated with 28-year-old Megan Faulkner Brown, the married young mom who just recently started in 2009 the successful Sweet Tooth Fairy Bake Shop in Provo, Utah. The gourmet bake shop's specialty is cupcakes. I sampled only her award-winning double-fudge cake bites, and I'm pretty sure I died and went to heaven for a few seconds. I discovered her business while reporting on how to launch a cupcakery (truth be told, a personal aspiration of mine, too) and found her start-up journey quite compelling. Faulkner left her day job in marketing, depleted her savings account, and got a loan from her grandmother to open the store. And all during a recession, no less. Risky? You bet, since some critics say the nationwide cupcake bubble will soon go the way of the dinosaur or the Krispy Kreme doughnut. And why leave the luxury of a job (i.e., a guaranteed salary and benefits) with so much uncertainty in the market?

Megan understood the high risks, but her entrepreneurial spirit and hard work eventually paved the way to profits in less than a year. As it turned out, a recession was a fabulous time to start a cupcake shop. As Megan explained to me, people were willing to still spend money on small luxuries that made them feel good. "Sure, maybe no vacation to Hawaii, but they'll pay $2.25 for a cupcake," she laughed.

There's a lot we can learn from entrepreneurs, and it's not just how to, say, launch a Fortune 500 company or a bakery in the Midwest. It's not always about following a path toward making millions or billions of dollars. Rather, it's about pursuing their passion for creativity, strong work ethic, independence, appetite for risk, and willingness to go the extra mile and down the road less traveled. Theirs are the attributes and behaviors we should all embrace for the great sake of enriching our lives and our bank accounts.

For my parting chapter in *Be Money Smart*, I've chosen to introduce this idea of embracing the entrepreneurial mind and spirit and to examine how to be a pioneer in life. Bottom line: It all starts with your willingness to take a chance.

A New Era of Entrepreneurship

Why are more and more Americans starting their own businesses or, at the minimum, taking more ownership of their revenue streams? A key variable in keeping your financial foundation solid is earning enough money to keep your bases covered and to achieve your goals. Best-selling author and behavioral expert Dan Pink describes in his book *A Whole New Mind* that "artistry, empathy, taking the long view, pursuing the transcendent…will increasingly determine who soars and who stumbles." He describes it as a revolution. Before, "left-brained" or binary thinking, also known as SAT- and CPA-style aptitude, "drove the world." Why the transition now? Abundance, Asia, and automation have diminished the importance of left-brain thinking, says Pink. In other words, we have so much that we now have a heightened sense of "need," we face fierce competition, and the electronic world is diminishing the value of left-brained skills. The world around us is changing, and we need to adapt.

The once-stable career path of working for one company and cashing out at age 65 is no longer a likelihood. Day jobs have become unpredictable. A job loss can seriously set you back *unless* you have set some protocols in place, one of which is entrepreneurship.

In a conversation with Richard Bolles, author of the famous career guide *What Color Is Your Parachute* and the new book *The Job-Hunter's Survival Guide*, he tells me that there is no such thing as an "essential" employee. The recession taught us that much, at least. "There is no safety in the structure of company or job market," says Bolles. "There are too many different waves of change in the market to make any person's job indispensable."

Having an entrepreneurial project is also food for the soul. Our day jobs may not offer enough money or the right kind of emotional fulfillment. Therefore, to really be financially secure, you have to put some or all of your earnings potential into your own hands. It helps to have a stream of revenue that you can control—either in lieu of or in addition to your traditional 9 to 5 income.

But, what if you have no fear of losing your job. Instead, you're worried that an annual raise and a bonus are not on the horizon. In that case, you might want to seek this alternative route to fulfilling your earnings aspirations. Perhaps you want extra money for a down payment on a second home, to renovate your existing kitchen and bathrooms, you may want to boost your retirement savings, send your children to private school; making some money on the side is a strategy you can control.

What if you want to transition out of your current job altogether and pursue running your own business full time—which could not only bring in more money, it will make you happier. Baby steps in entrepreneurship can build that bridge. It's not false to believe that entrepreneurship will make us happier human beings. That's not just my intuition talking. An early 1990s study conducted by researchers at Dartmouth College and the London School of Economics titled "Entrepreneurship, Happiness and Supernormal Returns," concluded that "the self-employed report significantly higher levels of well-being than employees." Why is that?

For one, when you are your own boss, you don't have the same fears as when you are employee number 4,352. Namely, the fear of job security goes away. Sure, start-ups and small businesses fail, but knowing you have the power and control to turn things around helps keep your spirits high and your focus clear. I'll never forget what one young, daring entrepreneur told me in 2009, in the heat of the recession, as she was transitioning from pink slip recipient to full-time, self-employed caterer. Passion for food was one motivator. Fear was the other. "I have a huge fear of failure," she said. "So I know I'll work as hard as I can to not fail. I have no other choice." And that's the truth.

More and more people transition to entrepreneurship because they are seeking a higher purpose and more happiness in life. As the market begins to settle, becoming your own boss may be less an economic choice and more a decision based on how you want to live your life.

When the economy came to a shrieking halt during the previous recession, entrepreneurship went full speed ahead for both men and women, as discussed earlier in this book. Men continued to start businesses in droves while women set records with their trailblazing (and now constitute more than 50% of new start-ups). Ladies Who

Launch, a savvy network that attracts young female entrepreneurs (both budding and established), boasts more than 70,000 registered subscribers in the United States and Canada. That's up from just 500 in 2005 when the group launched.

We've been over the *why* behind this trend. When companies are laying people off and the job market is weak, becoming your own boss is a viable alternative fully within your control. Now let's explore the *how* to transition to entrepreneurship and begin taking control of your career.

The Part-Time Entrepreneur

Anyone can be a part-time entrepreneur. After all, that role doesn't require that you leave your day job. And as uncertain as the job market is, one could argue that it's pretty crazy to leave a stable job while unemployment is setting generational records. Dr. Patricia Greene, the F.W. Olin Distinguished Chair in Entrepreneurship at Babson College, explained to me that "entrepreneurship is leadership." It doesn't mean dropping your corporate life to start a jewelry business or a restaurant. It may or may not mean owning a business at all. In its purest form, an entrepreneur is one who takes initiative, creates his or her own opportunities, and accepts some risks. It's somebody who wants to be in charge and earn freedom, flexibility, and control over his or her career and finances. And being entrepreneurial can lead you to a more fulfilling life and secure future.

So in this section, let's look at keeping the day job while pursuing something more interesting (and entrepreneurial) on the side. You'll know when you're ready to make the full transition to You Inc. (which we explore later, as well). In the meantime, here's how to get started.

Step 1: Remember Who You Were

Earlier this year, I went on the CBS *Early Show* with my tips on how to "monetize your skills." We all have skills and passions, I explained, but we don't bank on them as much as we can. Life gets so hectic that we forget what we really enjoy doing, what our hobbies once were, and what we're actually really talented at doing. So to begin, think about what you enjoyed doing in high school. Were you in the school play? Did you play saxophone? Did you volunteer? The first step toward entrepreneurship is self-rediscovery. It's recognizing what you truly enjoy doing (i.e., your passion), which is often rooted in child-hood and adolescence, when the world was a simpler place.

By following through with something you really enjoy, you will perceive it less as a "job" and more of a "lucrative hobby." I had the pleasure of meeting Erika Weltz Prafder, a *New York Post* columnist and author of a terrific book called *Keep Your Paycheck, Live Your Passion*. After years of writing about entrepreneurs and small busi-ness owners, Erika was able to brilliantly translate that entrepreneur-ial *je ne sais quoi* for the masses. It's hard to pursue your dreams full time, she explains, but a part-time commitment is far more doable and can just as well fulfill your creativity and lead you to making more money. She will tell you that a big part of discovering your "passion" is tapping into your earliest memories. She asks people to examine what they enjoyed doing back then. What were your aspirations? Was it to be a dancer, a singer, an actor? What were your extracurricular activi-ties? And more important, what were your dreams? It's time to pay attention, she says, because dreams—what she calls "windows to our souls"—are a lot more telling than we might think.

All said, some people are perfectly happy pursuing a side gig that just functions as a way to pay the bills and nothing more. My high school friend Allison is one such example. Allison works full time as an analyst for a web firm, and in her spare time offers social media help to promote musical companies and their national tours. She doesn't see herself turning this into a full-time career, but she's com-mitted to the job because it brings in an extra $10,000 a year and helps her pay down debt and afford large purchases like new tires or ski passes.

Fair enough. Keeping things strictly business is definitely an aspect of entrepreneurship. The ideal, however, is to make extra money and be passionate about what you're doing. But if you find a job that you can do, that fits well into your schedule, and that pays well…don't let me be the one to stop you!

Step 2: Channel the Urge

To incorporate entrepreneurship into your life, you need to get some *fire in the belly*. You need a purpose, a reason to pursue this goal. A layoff, dissatisfaction at work, a need to make more money to either pay for your needs (rent, utilities, debt, savings) or your wants (vacations, a new car, more clothes) are all stimuli for rethinking the composition of your work life. Imagine how as you create more opportunities for yourself your life might change for the better. Channel those thoughts of gaining financial security and happiness in your work life and stoke those flames of ingenuity.

Dr. Greene describes this fiery urge to be our own boss as "necessity entrepreneurship." On the one hand, it may be, "I lost my job and I have to do something," she explains. On the other hand, if you still have your job, you may feel unfulfilled or not earn as much money as you need, she says. In those cases, too, people are "needing" entrepreneurship to fill the gap.

In 2004, 29-year-old Amanda Cox began doubling as a chocolate maker and a marketing coordinator for a manufacturing firm in Cambridge, Ohio. Can you guess which was her day job? Chocolate has always been her passion. "I made it growing up," she said. "My whole family made chocolates." Following college, Amanda lived in an Amish county, where she gained more experience, and soon she began monetizing her skills, while choosing to keep her full-time job at the factory (for the much-needed income, health benefits, and paid vacation). Amanda managed her side gig online through her website NothingButChocolate.com. On weekends, she worked at festivals and events; she picked up a few wholesale clients mainly through word of mouth. For her, this part-time entrepreneurial endeavor served a couple of purposes: extra revenue to pay the bills and a passionate escape from her daily corporate responsibilities. Continue reading to learn what happened next!

Step 3: Make It Work

As *Project Runway*'s fashion consultant Tim Gunn would say, "Make it work!" For budding entrepreneurs, it's about putting your passion to work and pursuing it in such a way that you manage your time and money well. It might also mean "leaving the door open" for the possibility of turning your side business into a full-time business someday.

So, now that you've identified a list of things you enjoy doing, which of those activities can you realistically pursue in your free time? How you can turn it into a worthwhile extra revenue stream, all while maintaining your professional 9 to 5? I find that networking on Facebook, Twitter, and LinkedIn is a great way to start a word-of-mouth alert about the kind of work you're seeking. My friend Tim just started teaching English as a second language to young kids in the Toronto area. Full time, he runs his own magazine called *Corduroy*—so I guess that makes him a double entrepreneur?

Entrepreneur Tim: Corduroy and ELS

Here is how my hard-working friend is "making it work," in his own words:

I knew I wanted something flexible that allowed me to be my own "boss" and also something that paid well. With that in mind, I ruled out serving tables, retail, office jobs, etc. I've always loved working with kids (ever since my early days as a camp counselor during summers off in high school), and I have a ton of experience and education in writing, so I figured I would make a good English tutor.

> *I posted a couple ads online (Craigslist and such), but most of my students have come from referrals from family and friends. I also find it helps to be proactive: I'm not ashamed to tell people I'm tutoring or to ask them for referrals when I'm out for dinner, at church, at the mall, even at the bar! And believe it or not, someone will always know someone who knows someone. The trick is to talk up your experience (I find having a magazine and a Master's degree from Columbia University helps!) and also stay firm on your rate. I charge $40/hour. And because I don't waver or give discounts, people think/know that I'm worth it and they have confidence in my abilities.*
>
> *Right now I have 10 students, which puts an extra $400 into my wallet at the end of every week. It's not that much work either... 10 hours of actual teaching and then a couple hours preparing worksheets, lesson plans, readings, etc. I schedule the sessions around my magazine workload and it's worked out pretty well so far. Since kids don't normally get home from school until after 3 p.m., I have the whole morning to work on* Corduroy *and then spend the evenings tutoring.*

Whether you have one or a few side jobs, time management is really important. Some, like my friend Barrie, say you almost need to be "compulsive" about planning your time well. Barrie works full-time as an academic administrator and spends her nights, weekends, and summers directing theater. "The trick," she says, "is to be a compulsive planner and have a fantastic system for organizing your schedule, your long-term calendar, and your to-do lists. It sounds boring and utterly unromantic to say that following your passions takes responsibility and practicality, but it is true."

To help make it work, keep these following things in mind:

Avoid discussing your side gig at your real job in the presence of managers. Of course, you might need to get some clearance before starting a particular side job, depending on the type of work it is. Make sure there are no conflicts of interest. For example, I needed to get the okay from my boss at the news station to be a columnist at a local paper, because I'd be working for two media companies that cover similar stories. In the end, I was allowed because my byline in the paper would mention I was an NY1 producer—free marketing for the station.

Once you're working this side job, don't blab about it at your 9 to 5. If your boss starts to sense that it's taking away from your focus at work, your next review might suffer. Bottom line: Do your best to keep the two worlds separate.

Keep track of your side earnings. The IRS requires that we claim all income, including any earnings from freelance work. So, in a separate folder, tuck away a record of any checks or cash that you receive so that you have that information available at tax time. In addition, to help reduce your taxable income, make sure to save all receipts for any purchases made to support your side gig—whether it's a computer, camera, stationery, baking utensils, and even gas to put in your car for side-gig-related travel.

Take advantage of the Web. Tim mentioned how he used Craigslist to market his business. That's just one example of how the Internet can help you get your side gig off the ground.

I recently interviewed Maria Thomas, the CEO of Etsy.com, an extremely popular online marketplace for hand-made goods, from jewelry to paintings to bags, pottery, and more. Using Etsy's existing templates, the site lets sellers showcase and sell their work online in a professional manner. Maria tells me that the Internet has officially broken down a lot of the barriers to entrepreneurship. In fact, with so much technical support and access from e-commerce sites like Etsy, Shopify, eBay, and Amazon and marketing platforms like Twitter and Facebook, it's more practical than ever to start a business online.

Online Entrepreneurship

Whether as a side or full-time occupation, the Internet is becoming the modern-day place for work. In a conversation with Elance.com CEO Fabio Rosati, I learned just how much freelance work is shifting online. His company is a thriving online job community where hirers and job seekers can connect on myriad web-based project assignments. The company's latest data shows Americans earned 45% more money online in 2009 than the previous year. "For millions of professionals, traditional career paths and even full-time employment are becoming less attractive and viable," says Fabio. "At the same time, technology, competitive pressures, and economic necessity are making online work increasingly attractive to businesses."

The top-earning skills on Elance are information technology, creative (design, multimedia, writing, translation), marketing (search engine optimization, branding), and operations (administrative support, data entry). A company report from January 2010 shows Elance has more than 100,000 active employers and more than 300,000 jobs posted in the previous 12 months.[1]

When it comes to taking the reins of your career path, think big and leverage the Web, Fabio tells me. "Those individuals who invest in keeping their skills up-to-date and learn how to effectively market their talent in this global online marketplace will thrive in the future."

Full-Time Online Freelancing

Twenty-eight year-old William Meeks from Pittsburgh, Pennsylvania, has been a full-time freelancer since 2008, running MeeksMixedMedia.com single-handedly and finding and executing 100% of his work online. Many of his opportunities arrive through Elance.com. He says his need to make more money to support his family prompted him to take his revenue streams into his own hands and the Web offered the quickest solutions.

Between having a second child and moving to a new home, he and his wife had exhausted most of their credit cards and nest egg just to keep the rent and bills current. He says his previous web design and video production job at a manufacturing company barely allowed him to make ends meet. He was only earning $11 an hour (with the promise of a raise in three months). When six months passed and that promise remained unfulfilled, he started exploring evening and weekend side jobs. He quickly found short-term web design projects on sites like FreelanceSwitch.com, Scriptlance.com, and Elance.com. The gigs paid about $15 an hour, almost 50% more than his day job. After some easy math, he and his wife decided he'd be better off quitting his day job, transitioning to full-time freelancing, and using the Internet as his vehicle to find consistent work.

The switch, he says, has been both professionally and personally rewarding. "For better or worse, it's all on me now," says William. "I don't have that constant fear of being fired for a silly mistake anymore. I also love the flexibility of my schedule. If my kids get sick or even if I just feel like taking a day off, as long as I meet my deadlines, I can do pretty much whatever I want. I will never have to choose between my loyalty to my family and my loyalty to my job." Working on a variety of projects has also given him more career confidence. "My portfolio is strong enough now that most of the time my clients give me quite a bit of creative control. They trust me."

And the best part about freelancing full-time? "There are a lot of perks, but I think the biggest one is that you never get bored," says William. "Sometimes when you are working one job at one company for years, the most creative part of your mind can stagnate from the repetitive tasks and goals as they recur quarter after quarter."

Julie Babikan would agree. The 37-year-old graphic design professional has been freelancing full time for the past year, right from her computer in her Chicago home. She admits that she wasn't convinced it was the best long-term approach to a career, mainly because she could hear her parents' nudging. "I have had the idea that people must have 'real jobs' ingrained into my head since I was very young.

Although my parents never discouraged me from being an artist, I was still told in a roundabout way that a job in a company with benefits, steady salary, and a future was the way to go." A layoff in 2008 from her corporate job was the turning point for Julie, and she began to view employment in a whole new light. "I think we are shifting toward an individual-based economy," said Julie, "turning away from corporate conglomerates that evolved after the industrial revolution, going back to our roots of individual-based services." She, too, began her online job hunt on Elance, receiving the first project she bid on, a PowerPoint presentation for a Harvard professor. "I started getting really creative with the presentations, adding animation and sound effects, turning them into educational entertainment versus your typical corporate boring PowerPoint presentations." She had found her niche and rapidly began winning more assignments.

"I love being my own boss...I no longer have to be on a train at 5 a.m. for the city, and not return until 7 or 8 p.m. My rush-hour traffic is two socks and a dust bunny. I can take a break and visit my family. My nieces and nephews know me.

"And who says the Internet keeps you isolated? It is definitely not lonely. I use Skype frequently, as it is very cost friendly for my international clients. I have made friends in Australia, Ireland, and France, as well as all over the United States. The Internet also lets Julie select quality assignments. "It's not about getting as many projects as I can. It's about choosing the right projects. It's about working for causes I believe in (like nonprofit agencies, children's welfare speakers, environmental causes, and animal rights). These projects keep me going. I am not without a loss for work now.

"Also, I am no longer afraid when my current project is nearing completion," says Julie. "The more I work, the more I get the opportunity to work. The harder I work, the better projects I receive. This has been the best, most exciting, adventurous year of my life."

Transitioning to You, Inc.

Going from employee to self-employed is not a straightforward journey, and it may seem there's no "perfect" time to launch. Perhaps the
most important things you will need at this time are willpower,
resourcefulness, and cold hard cash.

For some, the official transition happens after a layoff. In January
2009, Amanda, the owner of NothingButChocolate.com, lost her full-
time marketing job. She recalls a moment of paralysis followed by
clear determination. Instead of finding a new full-time position, she
took her severance (which was only two weeks of unused vacation
time) and mustered the courage to turn her hobby into a full-time
home-based business. "Chocolate is recession-proof," she says. "Plus,
I'm happier." Is the money flowing in? Not really, but she's finally
driven to pursue an occupation, and that will be her ticket to success.

Jessi Walter, a fellow casualty of the 2009 wave of layoffs, can
relate. After getting her pink slip from the now-defunct Bear Stearns,
the 27-year-old took her severance and her savings to launch Cupcake
Kids!, hosting cooking events for New York City children. "My business was born out of a major life change for me," says Walter. "If Bear
Stearns hadn't been bought by JP Morgan, I'm not sure Cupcake
Kids! would exist today."

Theirs is that transition Dr. Greene would call a "necessity," and
as these women became more entrenched in their businesses full
time, they would soon realize the endless opportunities their businesses engendered. A month into her business full time, orders for
Amanda's treats began flowing in. "Before [when working full time], I
was too bogged down to follow up on potential orders," she says.
"Being laid off was the answer to my prayers... It was a blessing in
disguise."

Still, for other full-time entrepreneurs, quitting their day job is
the only way out. But it needn't be a rash decision. For Sarah Farzam,

it took more than a few years of paltry pay and sleeping on her brother's pull-out couch for the 26-year-old California native to change gears and become the CEO of her own small business. Bilingual Birdies, the company she founded in 2007, offers foreign language classes to toddlers and young kids and teaches through song and dance. While she broke from the norm and quit her job to pursue her own business, her move was a calculated one.

Born and raised in Los Angeles, Sarah flew to New York City fresh out of UCLA in 2006 to become a school teacher in one of Brooklyn's crowded high schools, where hallway metal defectors and bloody schoolyard brawls were a way of life. Admittedly, she was pretty nervous about moving across the country and starting a job in a city where she had no friends.

Sarah made the trip, despite the potential drawbacks and $28,000 a year salary, to be a public school teacher in New York City. When it all was said and done and taxes were paid, her paycheck amounted to a paltry $400 a week—practically destitute for a young 20-something-year-old woman in the most expensive city in the country. How to pay bills, save, eat, and maintain a social life? Thankfully, her older brother, along with his wife, was generous in allowing her to stay with them for as long as she needed. Their house came with a built-in alarm clock called 2-year-old twins who would wake Sarah up in the morning by bouncing on her makeshift bed.

Fast-forward one year into Sarah's teaching life and we discover she is—to no surprise—burnt out, fed up, and broke. Instead of inspiring her students with the words of Shakespeare and instilling college ambitions, her days—as she feared—were spent playing disciplinarian to emotionally unstable kids and searching for enough pencils, textbooks, and chalk to get through her classes. The New York public school system is, in many ways, a broken system, she would later tell me. It would not be Sarah's fate to change the system, and certainly not while earning her tiny salary.

Months passed, and Sarah felt like she was just going through the motions of life—and not much more. Get up, eat breakfast, subway to school, get frustrated with students, earn measly pay. Repeat.

Sarah's life would change for the better but only after the night she spilled her guts to a friend over a plate of enchiladas at a local Mexican dive. Tired and frustrated, Sarah began imagining what sort of day-to-day job *would* make her happy, and more important, what kind of job would give her the motivation to rise out of bed (assuming the twins weren't enough of a wake-up call). She still wanted to teach, perhaps just not in the traditional classroom-type way. What would help her get off her brother's couch, and what kind of work would fulfill her goal to be financially stable and educate kids?

It took a few hours of soul searching, but in that crowded village café, Sarah began drafting the beginnings of what would ultimately be professional and financial independence. Her ideal job, she concluded, would let her integrate her existing skills of teaching, dance, foreign languages (she speaks English, Farsi, Spanish, and Hebrew), and work with young kids. Integration was key.

Now how to make the transition? She was flat broke and couldn't afford to quit her job at that point. Luckily, New York City is awake at all hours of the day, and Sarah still had her late-night college body-clock ticking. She put her energy to good use, and for the next six months Sarah continued teaching at the high school while bartending in the evenings. She managed to earn hundreds of dollars a night in tips, and with that extra revenue stream, she aggressively saved close to $15,000 in four months—enough to give her the financial confidence to quit her day job and focus on her business idea. It was also, more excitingly, enough to help her move out of her brother's living room.

Her financial instincts were right. As Rich Sloan, the co-founder of StartUpNation.com tells me, you don't need tens of thousands of dollars to launch a company. "It's not correct that it's expensive to start a business. The average requires $10,000 to get off the ground," he tells me, and that includes the storefront and materials. And with so many start-ups setting up shop on the Web to start, you might not even need as much.

What's more important to have is the fortitude and willingness to wear many hats. Today, Sarah is the CEO of Bilingual Birdies, teaching toddlers foreign languages through song and dance in rented spaces throughout New York City. She hopes to expand the business to other cities and grow the curriculum to include more languages. Sarah's days, of course, can be quite stressful—as she's in charge of the operations, marketing, and overall business strategy of Bilingual Birdies. She does it all. She'll never forget the time the elevator didn't work in the building of one of her rental spaces. She had to help parents carry strollers and babies up five flights of stairs. "But it's totally worth it," Sarah shrugs. "I'm so happy because I actually love what I'm doing."

Ironing Out the Finances

So now you've caught the small business bug. You want to turn your freelance work or side job into a full-time occupation where you call the shots. You've saved up $10,000, more or less. And mentally, you're there. My advice? Don't assume you have to quit your day job right away. After all, you may have savings to support the business, but do you also have savings to support yourself? Remember Sarah bartended her way to extra revenue to eventually help venture out of the teaching grind and off her brother's couch. I would never encourage you to quit working your corporate job if that would mean entering a world of financial uncertainties. Things may be going great for your weekend event planning business or catering gig, but do you have the financial means to be a full-time entrepreneur? Can you afford health insurance if you quit? These are just some areas worth thinking about.

Yes, entrepreneurship requires risk, but you can still be successful with prudence. Elizabeth Soule, 29, managed to launch her photography business on the side while working full time as a project manager at a design firm. After building a six-month nest egg, she gained the confidence to quit her day job and officially launched her business in late 2007, but it was only when she had her financial ducks in a row that she followed through on her exit strategy.

It's no fun having to live in your car, not unless you think it will make you stronger. That was the case with young entrepreneur John-Paul Lee, the 32-year-old Korean American founder of Tavalon Tea. In 2001, John-Paul fled from his management-consulting job in D.C. with the burning desire to launch his own tea company. Did he act in haste? If you call selling your condo, car, and stock options in one week, in addition to liquidating your 401k retirement savings and pulling out seven credit cards as hasty, then sure. "I think I took a more aggressive approach, and if I had to do it all over again, I would've started with a stronger and larger 'cash war chest,'" says John-Paul. "Money gets used up much quicker than you think in the world of business… The last thing any entrepreneur wants to do is get into a cash strap situation which can lead to poor decisions based on desperation."

But sometimes—even John-Paul will admit—there are invaluable lessons in taking risks and experiencing "rock bottom," as we've gone over in earlier chapters. It depends on your capacity and tolerance for risk, as well as your dedication to a Plan B (perhaps even Plan C). John-Paul was okay living out of his car for a while. Would you be? I once heard a saying that there is a certain luxury you gain when you know what it's like to be poor. Part of that luxury is to inherently know what it means to appreciate the things others so often take for granted in life. There is also the luxury of an unquestionable work ethic.

For some, that financial strain and desperation you experience as a result of breaking fast and loose from the corporate world to start a business may end up being what ultimately drives them toward success. As John-Paul reflects more on his journey, "I definitely learned this the hard way, but it did coerce me to be more creative, and it brought out the best in me." It also turned Tavalon into a multi-million-dollar brand in under five years.

Tips for Making the Leap to Full-Time Entrepreneur

Seek affordable loans. "Don't be intimidated that if you don't have a lot of money you're not going to be able to get off the ground," says StartupNation.com's Sloan. Banks might not be as generous as they once were with providing start-ups with ample capital. Friends and family represent one possible alternative resource. You can contract agreements with individuals with the help of a peer-to-peer lending site like VirginMoney.com. Second, he says the Small Business Administration at SBA.com is absolutely determined to provide loans. You may also want to consider tapping into the peer-to-peer market for micro loans. Sites like Prosper.com and LendingClub.com are pioneers in this alternative lending market.

Barter. It's not just a handy system from the Middle Ages. A *New York Times* story in 2008 titled "The Cash Strapped Turn to Barter" cited a more than 50% growth in membership at companies that facilitate barters, like the Itex Corporation and U-Exchange.com.[2] Remember, however, that the IRS does require you to record the fair market value of bartered goods and services. So, if a friend designs you a website for your business in exchange for you painting a room in his house, you must report the fair market value of what you receive as income (and what you pay [through barter] as an expense).

Establish emergency savings. One of the biggest questions I get from small business owners is this: How much should I pocket in case things get ugly? My advice is to save at least 10% of your earnings into a savings account until you have at least three months of your business overhead costs covered. Because entrepreneurs don't generally have a steady cash flow, save as much as possible and do it on autopilot, putting an automatic percentage into your bank account each month.

Scale back. Back to Amanda Cox, the owner of NothingButChocolate.com: While attempting to make her young business thrive, Amanda earns less income, which means she needs to cut out as many little expenses as possible. Small sacrifices can mean big returns. And because she's single, she says the stress is more manageable. "I have the stress of whether I'm going to pay the mortgage or gas bill or electric bill, but it's my stress only," she rationalizes. To simplify her finances, she canceled her Netflix and gym memberships. She began cooking more, clipping coupons, and stretching her dollars as much as possible. Her baking supplies? They come from Wal-Mart, the discounting giant. She's also keeping her car in the garage more, since living downtown offers easy walking access to most stores. She's even adjusted the thermostat in her house to 62 from 65 degrees during the winter (which also helps cool the chocolate faster). "A dollar here and a dollar there, it all adds up. It's about readjusting how you do things and they way you think."

---

[1] *Elance Quarterly Talent Report*, January–March 2010.

[2] Mickey Meece, "Cash-Strapped Turn to Barter," *New York Times*, November 12, 2008.

Conclusion

It almost goes without saying that we don't enjoy delaying gratification. We're a culture that desires the quick fix, the microwaveable meal, and five-minute abs. And while this book offers a long-term approach to building financial independence and wealth, I know some of you may still hope for a crib sheet edition, so in the spirit of kindness, I give you *Be Money Smart…by Friday*:

1. **Clean out your desk.** Remember the most common phrase when it comes to getting organized and clearing the financial clutter in your life: Where do I begin? Although there's a whole mental aspect to this, you can start by addressing the physical space in your home where you pay your bills and store your files: Clean out your desk. Start with the easy stuff. Keep receipts for big-ticket items attached to warranties for as long as the warranty covers (at least a year). Trash receipts for small purchases after a year. Shred documents that you no longer need that contain any personal information.

2. **Make a money buddy.** It's key to have a partner in your financial life who can knock some sense into you when you feel the impulse to spend. For me, this person is usually my mom. For others, it might be your best friend, sibling, or parent. Get this person's phone number on autodial in your cell phone. Relay your goals to this person so that he or she can help remind you of them when your judgment gets cloudy while gazing at those $400 boots.

3. **Reflect on the risks you've taken.** Examine the previous year and all that you've accomplished. Believe it or not, even the easiest decisions you made carried *some* risks. Take the time to acknowledge what those risks were and how you overcame them, from taking on a particular job to moving to investing. Life may become a little less frightening after you do this. At the least, realizing how we can navigate risk will help us make better, more confident financial choices the next time around.

4. **Create one personal rule of thumb.** As discussed earlier at the beginning of this book, we love rules of thumb. An absolute rule can sometimes help make the most complicated decision easier. Just like those on a diet might make a rule of thumb preaching "no sweets after dinner," having a financial rule of "no jeans above 75 bucks," for instance, can help keep you out of the designer denim boutiques and help keep your money where it belongs.

5. **Use cash.** Unlike credit cards, where the financial transaction is paperless and invisible, when we see money disappear from our wallets, we're less likely to spend frivolously and impulsively. This practice can save you an average 20% a year, according to credit experts.

6. **Call up a close relative.** Ask questions about what you were like when you were a kid. What were your interests? What was one of the funniest things you did? What was your temperament? What was the craziest stunt you ever pulled? What did the other relatives say about you? Understanding what makes us happy, how we define *rich,* and the type of "financial" personality we have—these things are often rooted in childhood and growing-up experiences. In addition to channeling your memories, it's sometimes helpful to see yourself through the eyes of others.

7. **Automate.** Be money smart by leaving the math to someone (or something) else. If your company is not automatically depositing your paychecks into a bank account, get help from human resources to do so. If you aren't automatically paying bills every month, set up autopayments with your bank so that you never miss a payment deadline. If you aren't saving automatically every month, link your checking account to a savings account and make a regular contribution every time you get paid.

8. **Track your spending.** With so many mobile applications out there to help us track our spending, this should really take just minutes to set up. The benefits of tracking your spending are priceless. Understanding how you spend and how much you spend is critical to understanding how you can better save your money. You may suddenly realize you're going to the ATM four times a week and paying $12 each week in fees, which might prompt you to look for fee-free ATMs in your neighborhood (and whaddayaknow, there's one a few blocks from your home). Or, you may see that you're spending $50 a month sending faxes from the local FedEx when you could just buy a fax machine for $100 and break even in two months.

9. **Get visual.** To see it is to believe it. Set up visual reminders of your goals and aspirations to help prevent detours along your financial track. If you really want to have fun with this, make a collage board of all the things that represent what's important to you: family photos, travel destinations, a bank statement showing your savings, and so on. In addition, use computer and phone screen savers that show your goals so that you are often visually reminded of why it's important to stick to your course!

10. **Identify your top three creative skills.** This is a tip taken from the last chapter on turning a hobby into a revenue stream. To get this show on the road, start by jotting down three skills

or hobbies you have that you are passionate about. Your passion for skiing can turn into giving skiing lessons once a week at your local ski range. A love of travel could lead to travel writing or a blog that offers travel tips. Your cooking skills could turn into a catering gig on the weekends.

And there you have it. Voilà!

INDEX

Symbols

401k plans, 18
   protecting after job loss, 145
401k plan administrators, 103

A

accountability, 101-103
accountants, 103
addiction, money relationships, 56
addicts, 56
advocacy. *See* being your own
   advocate
affordable versus unaffordable,
   112-114
analyzing price tags, 33
AnnualCreditReport.com, 89
apathy, 54
appearance, 83
Ariely, Dan, 30, 79, 114
autopayments, 185

B

babies, 17
   cost of, 147-148
Babikan, Julie, 174
Babycenter.com, 17
Bach, David, 88
balance, organization, 87
bank help, 92
Bank of America, free help, 92
Bank of Mom & Dad
   Danielle, 78, 81
   Julie, 60-62

bank representatives, 103
banking, savings accounts, 121
   CDs, 122
   interest rates, 121
bartering, 158
   entrepreneurs, 181
being your own advocate, 95-96
   Amy, 105-108
   cable, TV, and Internet bills, 110
   car insurance, 108
   cell phone bills, 109
   characteristics of, 97-102
   home insurance, 108
   tuition, 109
Better Business Bureau, 100
Bilingual Birdies, 177-179
Bolles, Richard, 165
Brixey, Marcia, 84
Brown, Megan Faulkner, 163
Brusuelas, Joseph, 15, 64
budgeting tools, 91
Buffet, Warren, 156

C

cable bills, 110
Cage, Nick, 24
car insurance, 108
cars, 147
   paying off early, 125-126
case studies, worthy, 127-134
cash, 113-114, 184
cashing out, 140-141
CDs, 122
celebrities, debt, 24